CREATIVE WRITING FOR KS3

A TECHNIQUE GUIDE

EOIN BENTICK

First published in 2021 by Accolade Tuition Ltd
71-75 Shelton Street
Covent Garden
London WC2H 9JQ
www.accoladetuition.com
info@accoladetuition.com

Copyright © 2021 by Eoin Bentick

The right of Eoin Bentick to be identified as the author of this work has been asserted by him in accordance with the Copyright, Designs and Patents Act 1988.

All rights reserved. No part of this book may be reproduced in any form or by any electronic or mechanical means, including information storage and retrieval systems, without written permission from the author, except for the use of brief quotations in a book review.

Image on Page vii (top left) & Page ix: Designed by stories / Freepik

Image, Page 5 ('Dystopia') Copyright © Nick Vidal-Hall. Licensed under CC BY-ND 2.0: https://creativecommons.org/licenses/by-nd/2.0/legalcode.
Source: https://www.flickr.com/photos/132918212@N04/21718244812

Image, Page 105 ('newspaper') Copyright © VV Nincic. Licensed under CC BY 2.0: https://creativecommons.org/licenses/by/2.0/legalcode.
Source: https://www.flickr.com/photos/blok70/32030163840

ISBN 978-1-913988-13-5

FIRST EDITION
1 3 5 7 9 10 8 6 4 2

CONTENTS

Introduction	v
Exemplar Piece One	1
Write the opening of a story about a strange beast	
Exemplar Piece One: Guidance	6
Exemplar Piece Two	16
Write about a time (real or imagined) when you, or someone you know, broke something	
Exemplar Piece Two: Guidance	20
Exemplar Piece Three	31
Write a descriptive passage based on the image on the following page	
Exemplar Piece Three: Guidance	37
Exemplar Piece Four	45
Write the beginning of a story inspired by an image	
Exemplar Piece Four: Guidance	50
Exemplar Piece Five	61
Write a formal letter to the Prime Minister asking for school to be optional	
Exemplar Piece Five: Guidance	65
Exemplar Piece Six	75
You own a footwear company. Write an email to send to your mailing list persuading the reader to buy your shoes	
Exemplar Piece Six: Guidance	79
Exemplar Piece Seven	88
Write a speech to give to your class about the importance of art	
Exemplar Piece Seven: Guidance	92
Exemplar Piece Eight	101
Write a newspaper article about something that happened in your local area	
Exemplar Piece Eight: Guidance	106
Language Techniques and Technical Terms	117

INTRODUCTION

This book will help you through any writing task that you'll be asked to do: creative, persuasive, informative, whatever it might be.

Whereas other revision books guide students from the ground up, starting with the building blocks of sentences and working upwards, I am going to be guiding you through some model answers. This way, you can get accustomed to what makes a good piece of writing. I'll be pointing out features that I use often and introducing you to some handy tips and tricks.

Even Shakespeare imitated others! Google Arthur Brooke's *Romeus and Juliet*, for example, and prepare to be blown away.

The best way to learn how to write effectively is through imitation. That doesn't mean that you should copy my whole sample pieces word for word; it *does* mean that you should practise using the techniques, structures, and, yes, maybe even some of the words and phrases that I use.

That's how language works: we copy things here and there from different people. The more people we copy and learn from, the more sophisticated our language becomes. This book gives you a whole treasure chest to pick and choose from.

Structure is extremely important when it comes to extended writing; you need to have a beginning, a middle, and an end. That is why I have divided each model answer into these three sections. If you take time to think of a beginning, a middle, and an end in the planning stage of writing, your writing will be so much better. All it takes is a couple of minutes and the process is absolutely key to creating a sense of structure.

There are eight chapters to the book, each dedicated to a particular type of extended writing. The first four cover creative fiction writing and the second four cover different styles of non-fiction writing to persuade/inform:

1. Creative writing from verbal prompt (story telling)
2. Creative writing from verbal prompt (something that happened to you)
3. Creative writing from visual prompt (description)
4. Creative writing from visual prompt (beginning of a story)

1. Formal letter
2. Advertising email
3. Speech
4. Newspaper article

At the beginning of each chapter, I give some general advice about the type of writing under discussion. Then comes my sample piece. After that, I break the piece down into a beginning, a middle, and an end, paying particularly close attention to the ways in which I shift between sections. I highlight language techniques, punctuation, vocabulary and explain what works.

At the back of the book, there is a vocabulary bank and a list of language techniques that you can use for reference. Top tip: Keep a list of good words and phrases! You will find it so much easier to write impressively if you've got some great vocabulary up your sleeve.

Beginnings of Sentences

One piece of advice that is important to keep in mind across all of your extended writing: change up your sentence structure. The following piece of writing is exactly the sort of thing that you should *avoid*:

> There was a small cat in the field. The field was big and had corn growing in it. The sun was red. There was a boy called Juan in the field and he saw the cat. He was scared but he didn't know what to do so just stood there. The cat just said miaow and it was fine. Juan sat down and texted his friend, Marlow.

The problem with this paragraph is that each sentence either begins with 'There was' or with a noun ('The field [...] The sun [...] He [...] The cat [...] Juan'). This is not interesting writing. If you catch yourself beginning all your sentences in the same way, throw in an adverb, or a fronted adverbial, or anything that takes away from the monotony of repeated sentence structure!

Reworked, the above paragraph might sound more like this:

> Hidden amongst the towering corn, a tiny cat lay peacefully in the wide, wide field, catching the last glimpses of the sun's red rays. Nearby, a boy called Juan was strolling through the crops when he caught sight of the sleeping cat. He froze. With a yawn and a stretch and a lazy blink, the cat let out a little 'miaow' and padded away. Immediately, Juan whipped out his phone to tell Marlow all about his first feline encounter.

This is by no means a perfect paragraph and the subject matter is a little strange, but you can see the difference when I change up the sentence structure. Almost all my sentences begin with either an adverbial ('Nearby [...] 'With a yawn and a stretch and a lazy blink' [...] 'Immediately') or adjectival ('Hidden amongst the towering corn') word or phrase. This brings added emphasis to the short sentence, 'He froze'.

So, what is an adjectival phrase or a fronted adverbial?

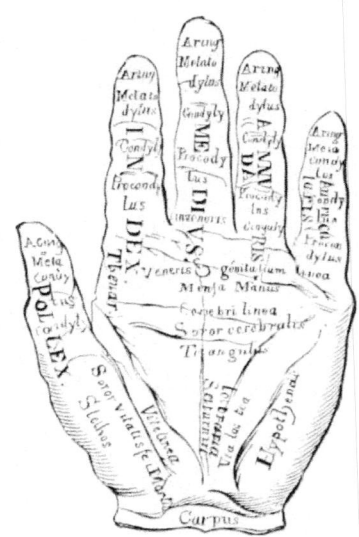

Remember: If you're going to write cheat notes on your hand, make sure you write them in a language you understand!

These sound pretty complex, but actually they are easy to get your head around. A quick way to understand them is that they are the bits that you put at the start of a sentence to make it sound more interesting. To be more precise, the fronted adverbial describes *how, when,* or *where* an action takes place. The adjectival phrase describes the subject of the sentence.

Fronted adverbials: 'Elsewhere...'; 'With a spring in her step...'; 'Above their heads...'; 'All of a sudden...'; 'Beyond the streetlight...'

Adjectival phrases: 'Blackened and oozing with sap, the tree…'; 'Proud of everything he had done, he…'; 'Bored of the blathering bleats, she…'; 'Glistening with gold, the dragon…'

Changing up the beginning of your sentences is a sure-fire way of improving your writing. Here is a really useful exercise that you should practise once a week:

1. Write a paragraph as quickly as you can.
2. Rewrite the paragraph, paying attention to the beginnings of sentences.
3. Note the differences between the paragraphs.

This way, you will start to feel the difference between a standard paragraph and one that is interesting to read. Remember: the form is just as important as the content. In other words, you could have a great idea for a story, but that would count for nothing if you did not use varied sentence structures to write it. In fact, often the simplest stories, beautifully written, are the best.

Put your energies into *how* you are telling your story, not what you are saying.

EXEMPLAR PIECE ONE
WRITE THE OPENING OF A STORY ABOUT A STRANGE BEAST

An imaginative writing question might ask you to write the beginning of a story based on a theme or a particular subject. In this case, you are being asked to write the beginning of a story based on a strange beast.

With creative writing, originality is key. But what *exactly* is originality? An original piece of writing is something you haven't heard before. It is unexpected. The pressure to be original might feel daunting, but there are some simple tricks that you can use to make sure that you are writing originally.

Originality in creative writing ultimately comes from the ability to imitate while also putting your own personal spin on things.

Firstly, think about a beginning, a middle, and an ending. In the beginning, set the scene; in the middle, shift the focus, the tone, or the perspective; in the ending, shift once more and try to resolve what you have introduced. These shifts are *very* important as they contribute to the originality of your writing.

Secondly, take time to say something in a different way. Pause, and actively think as you are writing: "Can I describe this more vividly?" In these pauses, ask yourself if there is an opportunity to vary the sentence structure, to use a literary device, to *show* and not *tell*. It sounds obvious, but you'll be surprised how often students just charge in and write the first thing that comes to their minds.

The artist Franz Marc's depiction of Caliban, the beast from Shakespeare's *The Tempest*. Like the beast in my story, Caliban blurs the boundaries between human and beast!

Thirdly, focus on descriptive detail. Take time to describe the sights, smells, sounds, atmosphere, weather. If the prompt asks you to talk about a beast, don't jump straight in with "The beast was ...". Set the scene.

Finally, think about narrative voice. In this task, you have the opportunity to adopt a third-person narrative voice. Will you be writing within a certain genre? Does your narrator have a character and opinions? Is your narrator omniscient (all-knowing)? Whatever you decide, make sure that you are consistent throughout your response.

 In the concrete badlands[1] of Greater Siltington, West Saxonbury, life was scarce[2]. Husks of an ancient civilisation tottered on bending beams that had been threatening to snap for decades. These antique blocks of flats, pocked and gaping and crumbling into the barren waste, were surrounded by little but desolation.

The air was as unmoving as the rusted vans that lined the streets – *thunk*. A boulder from the top of the tallest tower narrowly missed the masked head of Patroller 35701. She looked up and saw the tower lit up in the awful majesty of the reddening morning sky. Patroller 35701 winced; rain was coming.

Sixty-six floors up, the beast was prowling, panting, cogitating[3]. Distant clouds thickened. He watched the human clamber over rubble and old pipes, scanning the building as she came closer, ever closer. For five days now, he had been sheltering from the unrelenting sun without food, without water. He was usually much better at boulder-hurling.

No one wanted to survey the badlands, but Patroller 35701 was the kind of person who got the jobs that no one wanted to do. Back at headquarters, they received her scanned images over cups of tea and jokes about how grim it would be to be Patroller 35701 right now. But everything had to be surveyed.

Rain started to fall. She had been scanning for an hour and was only on the fourteenth floor. "Patroller 35701. Come in Patroller 35701," a crackled voice hissed in her ear.

"Copy. I hear you loud and –"

Sat at the doorway, between the dumbstruck patroller and the staircase, piercing her with bright yellow eyes, was the beast. It was hard to tell where the shadows ended and the beast began.

"Patroller 35701. Abort mission. I repeat: abort mission. We've detected movement in the building. You need to get out of there!"

The beast, not quite animal and not quite human, lurched towards her. Cowering, she held her hands up to protect herself and as a sign of submission. Again, the beast pounced, pinning her to the floor. He was panting heavily, thirsty and tired. As Patroller 35701 turned her head from the hot stench of his heavy breathing, she thought she heard him growl something that sounded uncannily[4] like, "Leave. Me. Alone!"

Before she knew it, he was bounding down the stairs and out into the early morning shower. Shakily, she stood up and dusted herself off. The red sun, still low in the one chunk of unclouded sky, blinded her as she stumbled to the window. Below, the beast bounded out from the building. He stood tall, threw his head back, opened his mouth wide, and screamed at the falling rain.

---

[1] ***Badlands*** – *dry, rocky waste land*
[2] ***Scarce*** – *in low supply*
[3] ***Cogitating*** – *thinking*
[4] ***Uncannily*** – *in a strangely unsettling manner*

EXEMPLAR PIECE ONE / 5

Really try to picture the image you're trying to conjure up. This, for me, is reminiscent of the badlands in my imagination. Copyright © Nick Vidal-Hall

EXEMPLAR PIECE ONE: GUIDANCE

Beginning

In the beginning, I set the scene. I focus primarily on the landscape. A scene is not set with one sentence, or two, or even three. Try to focus on one aspect of the scenario that is not necessarily linked to the verbal prompt. This will make your writing seem multi-layered. I decided to focus on the dilapidated buildings and the scarcity of life.

 In the concrete badlands of Greater Siltington, West Saxonbury, life was scarce.

- Avoided starting with the beast
- Invented a placename, adhering to the genre of science fiction
- Vocabulary ('badlands')
- Inverted sentence structure

EXEMPLAR PIECE ONE: GUIDANCE / 7

>> *It is important to demonstrate varied sentence structure. Since we might expect the sentence to read 'Life was scare in the concrete badlands of Greater Siltington, West Saxonbury', this sentence structure is 'inverted'.*

 *Husks of an ancient civilisation tottered on bending beams that had been threatening to snap for decades. These antique blocks of flats, pocked and gaping and crumbling into the barren waste, were surrounded by little but desolation.*

- Alliteration ('bending beams')

>> *Alliteration refers to the repetition of consonants.*

- Metaphor ('Husks', 'tottered', 'threatening')

>> *These are metaphors because the buildings are not **literally** the outer shell of seeds, not **literally** staggering around, and they don't **literally** threaten anything. This is a more subtle and interesting way to use metaphor than simply saying, "The buildings were husks".*

- Polysyndeton and rule of three ('pocked and gaping and crumbling')

>> *Polysyndeton is the use of lots of connectives in close proximity (... and ... and ... and ...).*

- The rule of three is a list three items, often the third item is longer or more descriptive (the rule of three technique is also called the tricolon)
- Extended physical description

Middle

Remember that the movement from beginning to middle requires a 'shift'. The shift that I have used is a shift in perspective, to that of Patroller 35701.

In order to create a layered effect to my writing, I also introduce a new theme that will recur throughout the whole piece: the changing weather. Peppering your response with the changing situation of something seemingly separate from your main action is a particularly effective technique.

My middle section is characterised by changes in perspective. This is to give you some examples of how to 'shift' effectively. I move from Patroller 35701 to the beast to headquarters and then back to Patroller 35701. This is probably the maximum number of 'shifts' you should allow yourself in the middle section.

I have also included a limited amount of direct speech towards the end of this section. Do not write much more direct speech than this. Once your imagination runs away with you, it is tempting to write as if you were creating a film script. You are not. Avoid 'He said' and 'She whispered'. Keep focussed on the physical, the senses, and the action.

 The air was as unmoving as the rusted vans that lined the streets – thunk. A boulder from the top of the tallest tower narrowly missed the masked head of Patroller 35701. She looked up and saw the tower lit up in the awful majesty of the reddening morning sky. Patroller 35701 winced; rain was coming.

- Simile ('as unmoving as the rusted vans')
>> *A simile compares one thing to another using 'like' or 'as'.*
- Onomatopoeia ('*thunk*')

>> *Onomatopoeia recreates a sound.*
- Punctuation use ('–')

>> *Using a variety of punctuation will be rewarded.*
- Change of perspective ('narrowly missed the masked head of Patroller 35701')
- Vocabulary ('awful majesty')

>> *Here, the word 'awful' is being used in an uncommon sense. Traditionally, the word 'awful' meant 'full of awe', and so 'awful majesty' comes to mean 'awe-inspiring grandeur'.*
- Sentence length and punctuation use ('Patroller 35701 winced; rain was coming')

>> *Using a mixture of short sentences and long sentences is highly recommended.*

 *Sixty-six floors up, the beast was prowling, panting, cogitating. Distant clouds thickened. He watched the human clamber over rubble and old pipes, scanning the building as she came closer, ever closer. For five days now, he had been sheltering*

from the unrelenting sun without food, without water. He was usually much better at boulder-hurling.

- Rule of three with alliteration ('prowling, panting, cogitating')
- Vocabulary ('cogitating')
- Repetition ('closer, ever closer' and 'without food, without water')
- Varied syntax (short sentence; very short sentence; medium sentence; medium sentence; short sentence)
- Humour ('He was usually much better at boulder-hurling')
- *>> This sentence refers back to the fallen boulder in the paragraph before, altering the reader's expectations of what has happened. The tone is informal and is suggestive of the beast's disdain for people.*

The beasts found in medieval art are perhaps some of the strangest you're likely to come across, and seem at once to be perfectly hilarious and perfectly terrifying!

 No one wanted to survey the badlands, but Patroller 35701 was the kind of person who got the jobs that no one wanted to do. Back at headquarters, they received her scanned images

over cups of tea and jokes about how grim it would be to be Patroller 35701 right now. But everything had to be surveyed.

- Shift in perspective
- Shift in tone ('kind of person who got the jobs that no one wanted to do' and 'cups of tea and jokes')

>> *The change from an ominous tone to a jovial tone releases some tension, allowing for the eventual meeting with the beast to be even more menacing. This particular type of humour is known as 'gallows humour' – a phrase that refers to the dark strain of comedy that stems from people's suffering.*

- Varied syntax

 *Rain started to fall. She had been scanning for an hour and was only on the fourteenth floor. "Patroller 35701. Come in Patroller 35701," a crackled voice hissed in her ear.*

"Copy. I hear you loud and –"

- Description of weather continues throughout action
- Short sentences increase tension
- Direct speech
- Punctuation use ('–')

>> *This is a great way to indicate an abrupt break in speech.*

Ending

The ending is the climax of the action. Even though you are only writing the 'beginning' of a story, it is important that you give a sense of closure to your reader. In my story, we realise that the beast, who initially seems aggressive, just wants to be left alone. There is a confrontation between the beast and the main character.

However, I decided to end the piece with a stark and vivid image that is somewhat ambiguous. Is the beast man or animal? Why does he scream? Such ambiguity is encouraged.

> *Sat at the doorway, between the dumbstruck patroller and the staircase, piercing her with bright yellow eyes, was the beast. It was hard to tell where the shadows ended and the beast began.*

- The use of the word 'dumbstruck' explains the use of the dash in the previous sentence
- The 'beast' comes at the end of the sentence, heightening tension
- Rather than saying 'The beast was difficult to see', I took a second to think about darkness and shadows and came up with a more original way of saying the same thing

EXEMPLAR PIECE ONE: GUIDANCE / 13

 *"Patroller 35701. Abort mission. I repeat: abort mission. We've detected movement in the building. You need to get out of there!"*

The beast, not quite animal and not quite human, lurched towards her. Cowering, she held her hands up to protect herself and as a sign of submission. Again, the beast pounced, pinning her to the floor. He was panting heavily, thirsty and tired. As Patroller 35701 turned her head from the hot stench of his heavy breathing, she thought she heard him growl something that sounded uncannily like, "Leave. Me. Alone!"

- Repetition ('not quite animal and not quite human')
- Verb use ('lurched', 'Cowering', 'pounced')
- Focus on smell ('hot stench')

>> *Always remember to think about the five senses (sight, smell, hearing, taste, and touch).*

- Ambiguity ('thought she heard')

>> *You want your story to make sense, but well-chosen moments in which the narrator or a character cannot*

make out what is happening can come across as sophisticated writing.

- Adverb use and vocabulary ('uncannily')

>> *Adverbs are an easy way to make your writing more vivid. However, because they are easy, they can be overused. Learn some interesting adverbs and use sparingly.*

- Punctuation use ('"Leave. Me. Alone!"')

" *Before she knew it, he was bounding down the stairs and out into the early morning shower. Shakily, she stood up and dusted herself off. The red sun, still low in the one chunk of unclouded sky, blinded her as she stumbled to the window. Below, the beast heaved out from the building. He stood tall, threw his head back, opened his mouth wide, and screamed at the falling rain.*

- Adverb use ('Shakily')

>> *Try to distance your adverb from the verb it is describing. 'Shakily, she stood up and ...' sounds better than 'She stood up shakily and ...'.*

- Verb use ('bounding', 'blinded', 'heaved')
- Multi-clausal sentences ('The red sun, still low in the one chunk of unclouded sky, blinded ...')

>> *Using clauses adds depth to a description and shows off an ability to construct complex sentences.*

- Asyndeton ('He stood tall, threw his head back, opened his mouth wide, and screamed at the falling rain')

>> *The opposite of polysyndeton, asyndeton is the use of lots of commas or semicolons without the use of connectives such as 'and' and 'or'.*

Human/beast hybrids appear in art time and time again.

EXEMPLAR PIECE TWO
WRITE ABOUT A TIME (REAL OR IMAGINED) WHEN YOU, OR SOMEONE YOU KNOW, BROKE SOMETHING

ANOTHER FORMAT for the imaginative writing verbal prompt might ask you to describe something, real or imagined, that happened to you or someone you know. If you can't think of a real episode, don't panic. Feel free to make it up!

Once again, originality is key. Focus on descriptions and building tension rather than "getting the story told". More than ever for these sorts of questions, don't let the truth get in the way of a good story. You are being marked on your storytelling, not on how accurately you can recount something that actually happened.

This prompt gives you the opportunity to experiment with the first-person. What is the character of your "I"? Will you be writing in the past tense, commenting on events in retrospect? Or will you write in the present tense, recreating thoughts and emotions through your language? The choice is yours. Try to give some character to your narrative voice.

How do we build tension?

Tension can be defined as the characteristic of writing that makes us want to read on. Tension keeps us on the edge of our seats, wanting to find out what happens next. Therefore, to incorporate 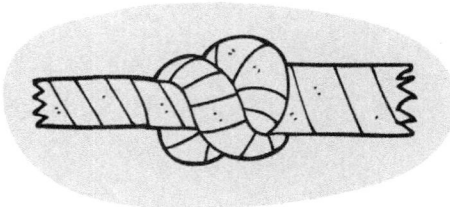 tension into our writing, we have to create a sense of something about to be revealed. We then have to delay revelation.

How do we do that?

With good old-fashioned description of course. Description takes time to read and so elongates the reading experience. What you will see from my story below is that the story does not have to be tense *in itself* for the writing to be able to build tension.

Remember everything from Essay One, too: think of a beginning, middle, and an end; *show* don't *tell*; and focus on descriptive detail.

 The forest glistened with snow on the cusp of melting. Occasionally, great chunks would slide and fall from the branches of pines, creating little undramatic snowfalls above our heads. We'd been walking for a good two hours now and only the thought of clattering cutlery, whistling coffee machines, and chocolate fudge cake was keeping us warm. That and the intellectual fire from our very important conversation about—I can't remember what—that had begun as soon as we left the car and was still raging.

Like a pair of busy mice, squeaking to each other through the undergrowth, we weaved through the forest trail. It was the first time my mother and I had gone out for a day trip for as long as I could remember, and it turned out we had a lot to say to one another. A change in scenery can do that, you know; there's always something new to say on a walk. Although, looking back on it now, all I remember is the snow, the enormous trees, the strangely furrowed[1] ground, the darkness of the deep wood—and the deer.

The day was bright; dappled light broke through the broad trees on the right-hand side and above us was cerulean[2] sky. To the left, however, was dark as a witch's grove, protected from light by the thick evergreen canopy above. In fact, that is the one snatch of conversation I remember: telling my mother that I was going to find the witches in the darkness and her marvelling at how quickly I disappeared into the blackness.

We laughed, we shouted, we sang. I banged sticks against trees and threw the barky remnants into the darkness. We were really cold now. The cake was just beyond the next bluff[3], down the hill, around the reservoir and suddenly ...

Silence.

It felt as if we had just stumbled across the lair of a mountain troll, who had heard us from a long way off. There was a shame in that silence; suddenly we saw ourselves from the forest's point of view, the forest that had waited patiently all this time for us to shut up and listen. There was no mountain troll and the forest did not judge. What there was, standing proudly before us, having leapt from the darkness to our left, was a tawny[4] brown deer. It lingered, lowered its head slightly, turned and sauntered away.

The silence left in the deer's wake was absolute. No birds called, no insects chirruped, we could not even hear the deer as it vaulted into the trees. The silence hung, pushing at me with a preternatural[5] urgency. My mother closed her eyes and took some deep breaths. I copied her, hearing my breath and my heartbeat at the centre of my head. The silence pushed harder. As biting as the icy breeze on my hands.

"Wow." I said, shattering the stillness with meaningless noise.

---

[1] ***Furrowed*** – *ploughed into lines; also the creases on a forehead*
[2] ***Cerulean*** – *deep blue*
[3] ***Bluff*** – *a steep cliff or bank*
[4] ***Tawny*** – *orangey-brown*
[5] ***Preternatural*** – *beyond natural*

EXEMPLAR PIECE TWO: GUIDANCE

Again, really try to picture the scene in your mind. This image is reminiscent of the scene as I saw it in my imagination.

Beginning

In this opening paragraph, I introduce three major themes that will recur throughout the piece: the snow, the coldness, and the loud conversation. I do not, however, introduce my mother, the deer, or the silence that the deer

EXEMPLAR PIECE TWO: GUIDANCE / 21

instils. This is because I want to heighten the tension; the detailed description keeps the story at bay.

Note also that instead of thinking of a physical object being broken, I took some time to think about something abstract: silence. I would highly recommend thinking outside the box like this. Take your time and try to write about something that you don't think other people will write about.

> *The forest glistened with snow on the cusp of melting.*

- Focus on scenery, thereby drawing the reader into the story
- Vocabulary ('cusp')

> *Occasionally, great chunks would slide and fall from the branches of pines, creating little undramatic snowfalls above our heads.*

- Multi-clausal sentence provides greater detail
- Adjective choice ('undramatic' – understated, adding to the serene imagery)

 *We'd been walking for a good two hours now and only the thought of clattering cutlery, whistling coffee machines, and chocolate fudge cake was keeping us warm.*

- Alliteration ('clattering cutlery')
- Rule of three ('clattering cutlery, whistling coffee machines, and chocolate fudge cake')

 That and the intellectual fire from our very important conversation about—I can't remember what—that had begun as soon as we left the car and was still raging.

- Informal tone ('That and …')
- \>\> Using a slightly more informal tone can help to make your first-person narrative seem more vivid; it helps to create a sense of voice.
- Metaphor ('intellectual fire […] 'raging')
- Punctuation use ('—')
- Authorial insertion ('I can't remember what')

Middle

In this middle section, I introduce the character of my mother and spend more time detailing the loud conversation we had in the forest. The mention of the darkness and the witch's grove brings an element of suspense to the story. There is a contrast between the eerie forest and the laughs of myself and my mother. The middle sections

end with the sudden intrusion of silence onto a scene that had been full of noise.

 *Like a pair of busy mice, squeaking to each other through the undergrowth, we weaved through the forest trail. It was the first time my mother and I had gone out for a day trip for as long as I could remember, and it turned out we had a lot to say to one another.*

- Simile ('Like a pair of busy mice ...')
>> *This simile makes myself and mother seem small and helps the reader to imagine the two characters walking among the immense forest.*
- Vocabulary ('undergrowth')

 *A change in scenery can do that, you know; there's always something new to say on a walk.*

- Authorial opinion presented as fact
>> *This gives the narrative voice more of a character; in this case, the narrative voice seems particularly interested in the benefits of walking.*
- Colloquialism ('you know')
>> *A colloquialism is a word or a phrase that you would tend*

to use in speech rather than written English.
>> *Its function here is to give character to the narrative voice.*
- Aphoristic ('there's always something new to say on a walk')
>> *Aphoristic means that something sounds like a saying or a proverb.*

> *Although, looking back on it now, all I remember is the snow, the enormous trees, the strangely furrowed ground, the darkness of the deep wood—and the deer.*

- A reminder of the speaking voice ('looking back on it now')
- Asyndeton
- Vocabulary ('furrowed')
- Heightened tension ('– and the deer')

> *The day was bright; dappled light broke through the broad trees on the right-hand side and above us was cerulean sky. To the left, however, was dark as a witch's grove, protected from light by the thick evergreen canopy above. In fact, that is the one snatch of conversation I remember: telling my mother that I was going to find the witches in the darkness and her marvelling at how quickly I disappeared into the blackness.*

- Punctuation use ('The day was bright; dappled light broke...')

>> *The use of the semicolon breaks up the flow of the sentence, drawing attention to the brightness of the day.*

- Vocabulary ('cerulean')
- Punctuation use (':')
- Juxtaposition

>> *I contrast brightness and noise with eerie darkness.*

- Simile ('dark as a witch's grove')

> *We laughed, we shouted, we sang. I banged sticks against trees and threw the barky remnants into the darkness. We were really cold now. The cake was just beyond the next bluff, down the hill, around the reservoir and suddenly ...*
>
> *Silence.*

- Rule of three ('We laughed, we shouted, we sang.')

>> *This repetitive short sentence gives a sense of being carefree.*

- Ominous tone ('We were really cold now')
>> *This time, the short sentence gives a sense that the cold is all that the character can think about. It is as if all the noise was to keep the cold at bay.*
- Asyndeton ('just beyond the next bluff, down the hill, around the reservoir)
>> *The asyndeton gives a sense of the character's rapid thought process, as he thinks himself towards the café.*
- Ellipsis ('and suddenly …')
>> *The use of the ellipsis makes the reader pause.*
- One-word sentence, visibly separated from the preceding paragraph ('Silence')
>> *This draws attention to the importance of the word.*

Ending

At this point, continuing with imagery drawn from fantasy literature, I create a feeling that is at odds with what has come before. I shift perspective, focusing on the forest as a whole regarding me and my mother.

The penultimate (second to last) paragraph of the story treats silence in a surprising way, suggesting that it caused some sort of discomfort for the narrator. This strange ambiguity adds to the intrigue of the ending.

Finally, I combine the oppressiveness of the silence with the coldness previously mentioned to bring about the breaking of the silence at the end.

As with the previous imaginative writing piece, the ending is unexpected. Usually, silence is thought of as peaceful, but here I have suggested it is uncomfortable. Again, writing something unexpected is highly recommended.

> *It felt as if we had just stumbled across the lair of a mountain troll, who had heard us from a long way off. There was a shame in that silence; suddenly we saw ourselves from the forest's point of view, the forest that had waited patiently all this time for us to shut up and listen.*

- *Imagery from fantasy ('mountain troll')*
- *Abstract thought ('there was a shame in that silence')*

>> *Whilst you should always be thinking of concrete images, it can be good to think of interesting ways to include abstract ideas.*

- *Punctuation use (';')*
- *Perspective shift ('suddenly we saw ourselves from the forest's point of view')*
- *Personification ('the forest that had waited for us patiently all this time ...')*

>> *Personification is when you give human characteristics or behaviours to non-human objects or animals.*

> *There was no mountain troll and the forest did not judge. What there was, standing proudly before us, having leapt from*

the darkness to our left, was a tawny brown deer. It lingered, lowered its head slightly, turned and sauntered away.

- *Delayed main clause ('What there was, standing proudly before us ...')*
>> *This is a classic case of building tension within a sentence. The deer comes right at the end of the sentence after two clauses that describe it.*
- *Anti-climax ('It lingered, lowered its head slightly, turned and sauntered away.')*
>> *Having mentioned the deer a couple of times before, I made it seem as if the interaction with the deer would be the climax of the story. However, with these subtle movements separated with commas, the encounter seems uneventful.*

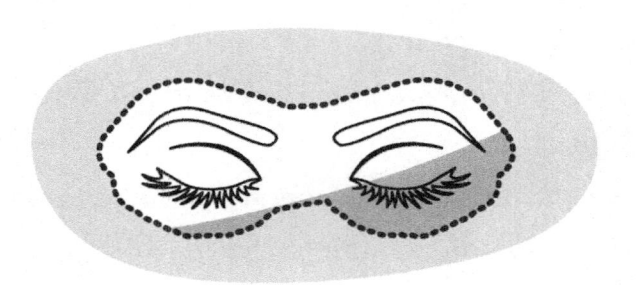

" *The silence left in the deer's wake was absolute. No birds called, no insects chirruped, we could not even hear the deer as it vaulted into the trees. The silence hung, pushing at me with a preternatural urgency. My mother closed her eyes and took some deep breaths. I copied her, hearing my breath and my heartbeat at the centre of my head. The silence pushed harder. As biting as the icy breeze on my hands.*

- *Repetition ('The silence [...] The silence [...] The silence')*

>> *The silence begins every other sentence. This gives the impression that the narrator's attention, no matter how hard he tries to distract himself, keeps on coming back to the silence.*
- *Repetition ('No birds called, no insects chirruped')*
>> *The repetition of 'no' emphasises the absoluteness of the silence.*
- *Vocabulary ('preternatural')*
- *Verb use ('pushing at')*
>> *Gives more of a sense of repeated pressure than just 'pushing'.*
- *Discrepancy between the sense of urgency in the narrator's head and the calm of the mother*
- *Unconventional syntax ('As biting as the icy breeze on my hands.')*
>> *This is not a proper sentence as it does not have a verb. Here, it gives a sense of how overwhelmed the narrator is with both the silence and the cold.*

"*Wow!" I said, shattering the stillness with meaningless noise.*

- *Limited use of direct speech*
>> *Always good to cut down on direct speech.*
- *Metaphor ('shattering the stillness')*
- *Short paragraph*
>> *Draws attention to the way in which the noise breaks the silence of the previous paragraph.*

30 / CREATIVE WRITING FOR KS3

EXEMPLAR PIECE THREE
WRITE A DESCRIPTIVE PASSAGE BASED ON THE IMAGE ON THE FOLLOWING PAGE

32 / CREATIVE WRITING FOR KS3

This image can be seen on this edition's back cover in colour!

THE DESCRIPTIVE PASSAGE is your opportunity to show off. Use all the techniques under the sun: metaphor, alliteration, tricolon, repetition, simile, onomatopoeia … you name it!

It can seem like a daunting task because you might think, "How can I write so much about one image? there's only so much there!" Well, you'll be surprised. Try to engage with every single aspect of the picture. Really squeeze the image dry.

Also, bear in mind that you can do a bit of storytelling. The descriptive passage is actually a fantastic opportunity to think of perspective. Who is doing the describing? One technique that can really impress is to reveal the narrator towards the end of your passage. This can show ingenuity, creativity, and originality.

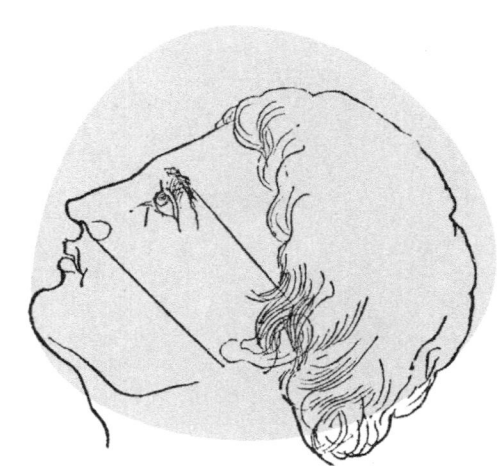

In your planning stage, a really handy trick is to write down all the words that come to mind when you look at each part of the picture. This is called "word association" and can help you to work out what it is you want to write about. Below is my word association:

Crows: caw, death, darting, ominous

Sky: skull, mottled, clouds, gauzy, grey, pale/dark

Houses: ordered, pointy, windows, old, European

Sign: direction, onward, upward

Street: slabs, graves, lead grey, bone white, clean, empty

Perspective: low down, wonky, something left on the floor, rubbish

From here, I then decide on what my main themes are. I want to do the description from the point of view of a piece of rubbish discarded on the floor. There will be a lot of deathly imagery in relation to the clean, orderliness of the street.

Finally, I want to think of an ending that will show a sense of structure. How about having a street sweeper coming and sweeping away the rubbish? Although there is no street sweeper in the image, I am allowed to use my imagination a little bit.

> From where I lie, the timeless town looms rigidly. The ancient angular brickwork lines up in narrow order, gesturing towards a skull-grey sky that is mottled[1] with gauzy[2] gaps of darkened blue. A comfortless glow radiates from the horizon.
>
> Across the dark pale sky, startled crows circle, soar, dart, and dive. Disordered, they paint a living picture across the neat and clean and tidy town; they caw[3], they flutter, they make a mess on the sterile streets and the deathly sky. Some call them harbingers[4] of death, but I see them as hardy cacklers of life.
>
> I lie discarded on the cobbles. I can make out leaden grey and bone-white slabs beyond, perfectly coloured for my

graveyard, my final resting place. A sign points onwards or upwards, either way I will not be following. Here I lie, rustling in the breeze.

Whirr, clunk, whirr, clunk

The breeze carries with it a strange mechanical noise from behind me. This must have been what startled the crows. As it gets closer and closer, louder and louder, its spinning brushes and unwieldy[5] motion can only mean one thing: street sweeper. I'm moving on.

Asleep, or breakfasting, or doing whatever it is that humans do in the mornings, the inhabitants of this antiquated[6] town will miss the unremarkable drama of a crisp packet being swept up. The boy who dropped me, sat by a magnificent arched window, watching cartoons as he wolfed down his sugary cereal, will not witness my sweeping. In twenty minutes' time, he will step out into his little life, breathe in the pine-fresh air, run his hands over spotlessly cold iron railings, follow signs that lead on, and hear nothing but the sound of little lives clacking on leaden grey and bone-white pavements.

For now, the streets are empty and no faces press at the windows. The sweeper is almost upon me and all I can hear is its endless churning, awkward trundling, and sporadic beeping; the noise of the orderly life. I wonder if the driver sees me, or whether he too cannot take his eyes from the crows and their dizzying dance.

But I guess that is the point: I am to be unseen. The sweeper gathers me and moves me out of sight. As clean shoes clickity clack on the spotless streets, I sit hidden amongst a mountainous pile of detritus[7]. Elsewhere, simply elsewhere.

---

[1] ***Mottled*** – *irregularly spotted*
[2] ***Gauzy*** – *thin and translucent (see-through)*
[3] ***Caw*** – *the noise a crow makes*
[4] ***Harbingers*** – *omens; signs of something to come*
[5] ***Unwieldy*** – *moving awkwardly due to size, shape, or weight*
[6] ***Antiquated*** – *old-fashioned*
[7] ***Detritus*** – *waste or debris*

EXEMPLAR PIECE THREE: GUIDANCE

Beginning

The beginning focuses on the town, the sky, and the crows. It is here that I use a lot of the imagery that I come up with through word association. I use dense sentences full of descriptive vocabulary, but I also vary my sentence length in order to create a vibrant passage.

> *From where I lie, the timeless town looms rigidly. The ancient angular brickwork lines up in narrow order, gesturing towards a skull-grey sky that is mottled with gauzy gaps of darkened blue. A comfortless glow radiates from the horizon.*
>
> • First person pronoun ('I')
> \>\> *Even though I do not make it explicit that the narrator is a*

crisp packet at the beginning of the passage, I do immediately make it clear that the piece is written from a particular perspective.

- Personification ('gesturing')
- Fronted adverbial ('From where I lie')

>> *Beginning sentences with adverbial phrases helps you to avoid always starting with a noun.*

- Sentence variety

>> *I have one long and complex sentence sandwiched between two short ones.*

- Alliteration and adjective use ('timeless town', 'skull-grey sky', 'gauzy gaps')

>> *These are some unusual adjectives that jump out at the reader and show a wide vocabulary.*

> *Across the dark pale sky, startled crows circle, soar, dart and dive. Disordered, they paint a living picture across the neat and clean and tidy town; they caw, they flutter, they make a mess on the sterile streets and the deathly sky. Some call them harbingers of death, but I see them as hardy cacklers of life.*

- Alliterative list of verbs ('circle, soar, dart and dive')

>> *This list gives a sense of the crows' erratic movements.*

- Metaphor ('they paint a living picture')
- Polysyndeton ('neat and clean and tidy')

>> *The polysyndeton accentuates the rigorous tidiness of the town.*
- Tricolon ('they caw, they flutter, they make a mess')
- Alliteration ('sterile streets')
- Use of first-person pronoun ('I')

>> *I remind the reader that the description is coming from a specific perspective.*
- Unexpected description ('hardy cacklers of life')

>> *By explicitly disagreeing with the way in which crows are otherwise seen, I create a special relationship between the crows and the narrator.*

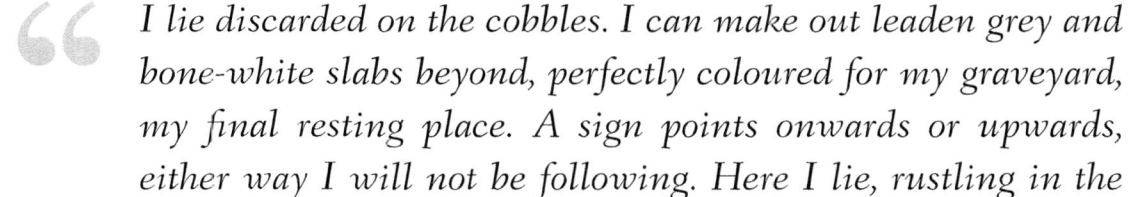

" *I lie discarded on the cobbles. I can make out leaden grey and bone-white slabs beyond, perfectly coloured for my graveyard, my final resting place. A sign points onwards or upwards, either way I will not be following. Here I lie, rustling in the breeze.*

- Greater use of first-person ('I')

>> *By increasing the use of the first-person pronoun, I shift*

the focus from the town to the crisp packet.
- Deathly imagery ('leaden grey and bone-white slabs', 'graveyard', 'final resting place')
- Repetition ('I lie discarded', 'Here I lie')

Middle

Once you feel like you have described everything you can see in detail, it can feel like you can go no further. This is, in fact, the most common pitfall for the descriptive writing task.

However, you *can* write more. Go back to your plan or go back to what you have already written and see what further connections you can make. In my head, I have made two routes that I want to go down: the cleanness of the streets and the fate of the crisp packet.

If you're introducing elements that are not in the original image, give them some thought — you want to use them well!

It could have been anything: I could have gone down a much more deathly route (considering how much deathly imagery was in my opening section) and described a plague-stricken scene; or maybe I could have talked about the oldness of the town or fact that it seems European; or I could have gone with the crows and thought about where they were off to, or what squabbles they were having.

Whatever it was, it would have helped me to furnish my middle section. Remember: there is always something to run with. You just have to go for it!

> *Whirr, clunk, whirr, clunk*
>
> *The breeze carries with it a strange mechanical noise from behind me. This must have been what startled the crows. As it*

gets closer and closer, louder and louder, its spinning brushes and unwieldy motion can only mean one thing: street sweeper. I'm moving on.

- Onomatopoeia ('Whirr, clunk, whirr, clunk')
- \>> *Onomatopoeia is one of those techniques you want to use sparingly, but when you do use it, it can help to recreate the moment.*
- Building tension
- \>> *I do not immediately make it obvious that this is a street sweeper; I keep that information hidden to the end of the paragraph.*
- Repetition ('closer and closer, louder and louder')
- Short sentence ('I'm moving on')

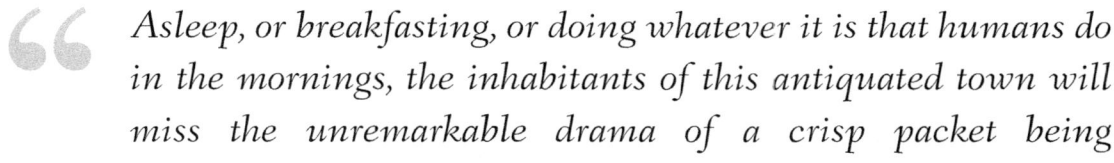

Asleep, or breakfasting, or doing whatever it is that humans do in the mornings, the inhabitants of this antiquated town will miss the unremarkable drama of a crisp packet being swept up.

- Change in perspective
- \>> *Moving to the inhabitants of the town, I now introduce a new perspective that enriches the image.*
- Polysyndeton ('Asleep, or breakfasting, or doing whatever')
- Vocabulary ('antiquated', 'unremarkable')

- Revelation of perspective ('humans', 'crisp packet')

>> *Although the importance of the street sweeper gives a hint, it is at this moment that the identity of the narrator is revealed.*

> *The boy who dropped me, sat by a magnificent arched window, watching cartoons as he wolfed down his sugary cereal, will not witness my sweeping. In twenty minutes' time, he will step out into his little life, breathe in the pine-fresh air, run his hands over spotlessly cold iron railings, follow signs that lead on, and hear nothing but the sound of little lives clacking on leaden grey and bone-white pavements.*

- Change in perspective

>> *Moving to the boy who dropped the crisp packet provides a backstory to the narrator and helps to establish the tension between the crisp packet and cleanliness.*

- Long, complex sentences

>> *Both sentences here contain multiple clauses. The long sentences recreate the crisp packet's thought patterns as it imagines how little the boy cares.*

- Sensory imagery ('pine-fresh air', 'spotlessly cold iron railings', 'clacking')

>> These descriptions cover the senses of smell, touch, and sound.

- Repetition of imagery ('leaden grey and bone-white pavements')
- Mixture of abstract and physical imagery ('little lives clacking')

>> This is a fun technique to try out. Throw together an abstract noun and a physical verb to create some really original phrases: 'my happiness cycled home'; 'his worries kept on bumping into everyone'; 'she planted her memories in the soft grass'.

Ending

The ending was always going to be the moment when the street sweeper sweeps up the crisp packet. However, I also wanted to include a final note on where the crisp packet finishes up. This allows me to compare the cleanliness of the town with the ugliness of a landfill rubbish dump.

> *For now, the streets are empty and no faces press at the windows. The sweeper is almost upon me and all I can hear is its endless churning, awkward trundling, and sporadic beeping; the noise of the orderly life. I wonder if the driver sees me, or whether he too cannot take his eyes from the crows and their dizzying dance.*

- Change of perspective again to the present moment
- Tricolon ('endless churning, awkward trundling, and sporadic beeping')
- Punctuation use (';')

- Quick change of perspective to the driver
- Alliteration ('dizzying dance')

> *But I guess that is the point: I am to be unseen. The sweeper gathers me out of sight. As clean shoes clickity clack on the spotless streets, I sit hidden amongst a mountainous pile of detritus. Elsewhere, simply elsewhere.*

- Change in tone ('But I guess that is the point')

>> *The crisp packet becomes more philosophical at the end here.*

- Punctuation use (':')
- Interesting adjective choice ('I am to be unseen')
- Alliteration ('clickity clack on the spotless streets')
- Vocabulary ('detritus')
- Verbless sentence ('Elsewhere, simply elsewhere')

>> *This is not technically a proper sentence because it does not have a verb. However, in creative writing, you can use a sentence like this for effect. Here, the effect is that it heightens sympathy for the crisp packet.*

EXEMPLAR PIECE FOUR
WRITE THE BEGINNING OF A STORY INSPIRED BY AN IMAGE

This image can be seen on this edition's back cover in colour!

DESCRIPTION IS DEFINITELY key when it comes to writing the beginning of a story. You will show off your language skills most impressively by taking the time to describe a scene in detail.

This is also the opportunity to think about characterisation. Who are the characters in your story? What are they like? How do they relate to each other? What do they want?

Remember that a story full of direct speech is never that good. You want to create character through description and action.

A particular method that I employ in my story is the alternation between the physical and the abstract. I flit between physical objects and the thoughts that they inspire. In this way, a rather simple tale is made to seem extremely important.

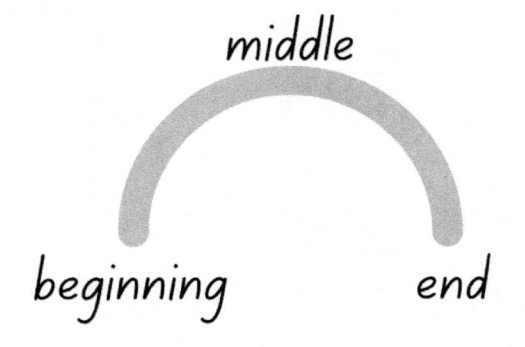

Although it is a story that seems to be about two girls playing in a tree, it is also about the long history of a tree through time. Again, this can be a useful story-telling technique: rooting a grand idea in a simple tale.

When I looked at the picture of the tree stump, I thought about how I could turn this static image into a story. My first thought was to fairies and elves. There is nothing necessarily wrong with writing fantasy literature, but it is much easier to fall into cliché and to adopt a more childish tone when writing about magical creatures. Often, the simpler the story, the more interesting the writing will be.

Once I had decided that I would write the story about a den for two girls, I had to think about what the narrative arc would be; what was my beginning, middle, and end?

Seeing the light and the leaves in the picture, I thought it would be good to begin with a summer setting. I could then establish the relationship between my two characters, Jess and Harsha, tired from the day's work but excited about what lay ahead at the tree.

The middle section would then focus on the tree, its history, and how Jess and Harsha enjoy it.

Finally, the ending would introduce the ominous chain, which I could just about make out in the image. As you can see, there is not that much action *at all*, but there is a great deal of descriptive imagery that draws the reader in.

> It was a bright summer's evening and the cooling air held a volatile[1] sense of wild abandon[2]. Walk-running to the great oak, Jess and Harsha inhaled this enlivening fuel in giddy gulps. They had spent the afternoon helping the farmer stack hay and, though the heat and the work had driven them nearly to exhaustion, the changing air was now filling them with that joy they had felt on many a long summer's evening, but which, at this moment, felt indescribably new.
>
> They laughed and hid and chased and argued and arrived, out of breath, halfway through a grave[3] discussion about the merits and shortcomings of being interested in things. The

oak was as it had always been—for as long as they had been visiting it anyway. It had in fact changed quite considerably over the seven hundred and fifty years it had been standing in Mayor Phillis' field. Of course it was wider, taller, leafier, and different in all those ways that you would expect a tree to be from an acorn, but in recent years (say, the past hundred) it had become roomier and somewhat stonier. Its bark, segmented like the scales of a dragon, was fossilising as its soft core was being eaten away by insects, fungi, and goodness knows what else! What remained was an aged arboreal[4] den, currently occupied by Jess and Harsha, the Queens of Fulsome Marsh.

As the sun fell, so the shadows grew; a distant tree stump was transformed into a towering totem[5] by the shade across the newly shorn field. The girls had just finished drawing up a manifesto[6] for the 'Interested Life' and Harsha was taking a stroll around the edge of the oak, taking in the impermanent gold of the evening while Jess was adding foliate[7] borders to their hallowed[8] document. Though the sky was changing second by second, moment by moment, Harsha felt like the universe was standing still for her—as if this instant were caught inside a swirling marble.

Heading back to Jess, her foot caught on something hard, and she stumbled into the stony bark of the tree.

"What is—Jess, come, have a look at this!"

With ink all over her hands and wrists, Jess poked out from the trunk's awning. She stepped out gingerly[9], her eyes fixed on the brazen[10] incongruity[11] of the metalwork in their natural haven. It was a black that shone and cast no shadow.

Someone had attached this ugly, deathly chain to the ancient tree.

They stood over the omen like mourners.

"You never know," Jess found herself saying, "It might be to protect it."

The sun had set. It was getting cold. The marble was now colliding with all the dark things kept at bay. It's times like these, Harsha thought, that you really needed a proper grown-up to tell you everything is going to be OK.

---

[1] ***Volatile*** – *unpredictable; capable of being set alight at any moment*

[2] ***Abandon*** – *a lack of restraint*

[3] ***Grave*** – *serious*

[4] ***Arboreal*** – *of or pertaining to trees*

[5] ***Totem*** – *a sacred object, often in the form of a tall, carved pole*

[6] ***Manifesto*** – *a written declaration of a person or organisation's intentions and beliefs*

[7] ***Foliate*** – *decorated with leaves or leaf-like images*

[8] ***Hallowed*** – *made holy*

[9] ***Gingerly*** – *in a careful or cautious manner*

[10] ***Brazen*** – *bold*

[11] ***Incongruity*** – *the state of being incompatible or out of place*

EXEMPLAR PIECE FOUR: GUIDANCE

Beginning

As ever, it is very important to set the scene with sensory imagery. I have decided to include a mixture of physical and abstract imagery, both of which are introduced through the senses.

I introduce my characters early, but don't spend too long describing what they look like or what sort of people they are (this would be telling and not showing). I let the characters of Jess and Harsha reveal themselves through their actions later in the story. At this point, the two characters share the same characteristics of being tired but excited.

> *It was a bright summer's evening and the cooling air held a volatile sense of wild abandon. Walk-running to the great oak, Jess and Harsha inhaled this enlivening fuel in giddy gulps.*

They had spent the afternoon helping the farmer stack hay and, though the heat and the work had driven them nearly to exhaustion, the changing air was now filling them with that joy they had felt on many a long summer's evening, but which, at this moment, felt indescribably new.

- Setting the scene ('It was a bright summer's evening')
- Abstract imagery introduced through the senses ('the cooling air held a volatile sense of wild abandon')

>> *This roots the feeling of excitement in the sensation of the cooling air, tying the characters' emotions to the setting.*

- Compound verb ('Walk-running')

>> *This demonstrates a creative use of language.*

- Metaphor ('enlivening fuel')

>> *Likening the cooling evening air to fuel again reinforces the idea that their excitement is linked to the atmosphere.*

- Alliteration ('giddy gulps')
- Long, complex sentence ('They had spent ...')

>> *Uses the pluperfect tense ('had spent'), a subordinate clause ('though the heat...'), and a coordinating clause ('but which...').*

>> *The pluperfect tense refers to something that had happened before something already in the past. The easiest way to remember the pluperfect is that is uses word 'had': 'she had already eaten her breakfast, but she*

EXEMPLAR PIECE FOUR: GUIDANCE / 51

was still hungry'; *'they had been friends for ten years before they discovered they were related'*.
- Narrative distance from characters

>> *There is a difference between what Jess and Harsha think (that this is a new feeling) and what the narrator thinks (that they have felt this before). This helps to establish the narrative voice and characterise Jess and Harsha as youthful and perhaps naive.*

Middle

It is in this middle section that I make it clear that the oak itself is a central character of the story. When Jess and Harsha arrive at the oak tree, I "zoom out" and start to think of the tree throughout its life before coming back to the present moment with Jess and Harsha.

This is a great technique to give depth to a particular story. Focus on an object or a peripheral character—or whatever it might be—and give it brief history. Try to make sure that the history you give is related to the central theme or plot of your story.

Just like in all my other creative writing stories, I have kept track of the changing weather in order to provide a sense of structure. It is such an easy technique, but one that can really impress your reader. It is in this middle section that the difference in the characters emerges: Harsha is more pensive and Jess likes to make things look good. I don't tell my reader this, I show it to them through the characters' actions.

> *They laughed and hid and chased and argued and arrived, out of breath, halfway through a grave discussion about the merits and shortcomings of being interested in things.*

- Polysyndeton ('They laughed and hid and chased and argued and arrived')
>> *The effect of the polysyndeton here is to recreate the breathless excitement of the girls.*
- Vocabulary ('grave')

> *The oak was as it had always been—for as long as they had been visiting it anyway. It had in fact changed quite considerably over the seven hundred and fifty years it had been standing in Mayor Phillis' field.*

- Punctuation use ('—')
>> *The use of this em dash (that piece of punctuation that looks like a hyphen, but is a little bit longer) creates a shift in the narration. It allows the narrative voice to move from the girls' perspective to the wider perspective of the tree's lifetime.*

> *Of course it was wider, taller, leafier, and different in all those ways that you would expect a tree to be from an acorn, but in recent years (say, the past hundred) it had become roomier and somewhat stonier.*

- Tricolon ('wider, taller, leafier')
- Informal tone ('and different in all those ways that you would expect a tree to be from an acorn', '(say, the past hundred)')

>> This light-hearted aside helps to characterise the narrative voice as one who has authoritative perspective on the lives of trees.

> *Its bark, segmented like the scales of a dragon, was fossilising as its soft core was being eaten away by insects, fungi, and goodness knows what else! What remained was an aged arboreal den, currently occupied by Jess and Harsha, the Queens of Fulsome Marsh.*

- Simile ('segmented like the scales of a dragon')

>> *Makes the tree seem even more ancient and mythical.*
- Tricolon ('insects, fungi, and goodness knows what else!')

>> *Vocabulary ('arboreal').*
- Made up placename ('Fulsome Marsh')

>> *This helps to realise the setting.*

" *As the sun fell, so the shadows grew; a distant tree stump was transformed into a towering totem by the shade across the newly shorn field.*

- Balanced phrasing ('As the sun fell, so the shadows grew')
- Punctuation use (';')
- Metaphor ('a tree stump was transformed into a towering totem')

" *The girls had just finished drawing up a manifesto for the 'Interested Life' and Harsha was taking a stroll around the edge of the oak, taking in the impermanent gold of the evening while Jess was adding foliate borders to their hallowed document.*

- Characterisation ('The girls had just finished drawing up a manifesto for the 'Interested Life')

>> *This is an example of* showing *and not* telling. *The fact that they have written a manifesto about being interested in life is much more effective than saying, 'The girls were interested in life'.*

- Character differentiation
- Vocabulary ('impermanent', 'foliate', 'hallowed')
- Multi-clausal *sentence*

>> *It can be good to show off your command of difficult sentences. Make sure that they are grammatically correct!*

" *Though the sky was changing second by second, moment by moment, Harsha felt like the universe was standing still for her—as if this instant were caught inside a swirling marble.*

- Repetition ('second by second, moment by moment')
- Simile ('as if this instant were caught inside a swirling marble')

>> *There is a mixture of the physical and the abstract here as*

EXEMPLAR PIECE FOUR: GUIDANCE / 57

I try to find a definite image to capture the idea of time standing still. I highly recommend being bold and trying out similes like this. As you try to find the right words, a nice image might pop into your head.

Ending

With the rest of the story having been fairly uneventful, it is in the ending where most of the action takes place. The tone shifts dramatically as the girls look at the chain and wonder what it means.

Visually, you can see the difference between the ending and that which comes before through the broken paragraphs and the presence of direct speech. I create tension by not immediately revealing the fact that the object Harsha has tripped up on is a chain.

I end with ambiguity, so that the reader is left in the same state as Harsha and Jess as to the reason for the chain being there.

> *Heading back to Jess, her foot caught on something hard, and she stumbled into the stony bark of the tree.*
>
> *"What is—Jess, come, have a look at this!"*

- Direct speech
- Aposiopesis ('What is—')
>> *This is just a technical term for breaking off mid speech. It can help to give a realistic sense of voice.*

> *With ink all over her hands and wrists, Jess poked out from the trunk's awning. She stepped out gingerly, her eyes fixed on the brazen incongruity of the metalwork in their natural haven. It was a black that shone and cast no shadow. Someone had attached this ugly, deathly chain to the ancient tree.*

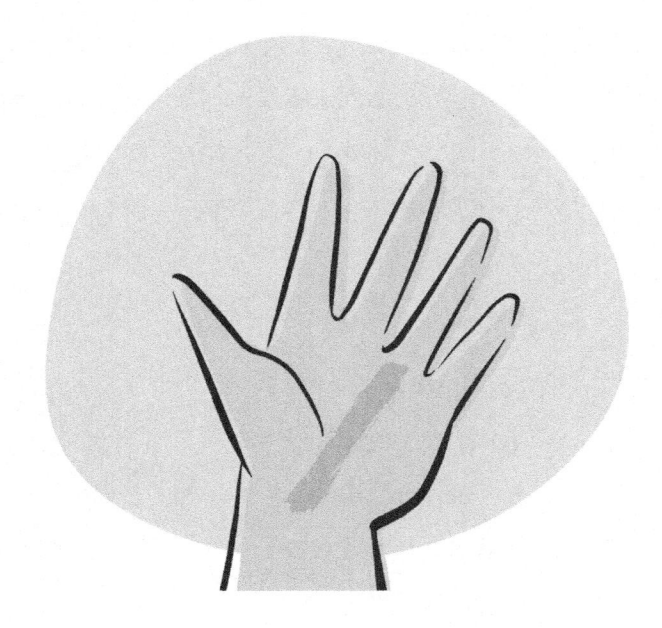

- Adverb use ('gingerly')
- Vocabulary ('brazen incongruity')
- Heightening tension

>> *Instead of explicitly referring to the chain, I use the word 'metalwork' to pique the reader's interest.*

- Short sentence ('It was a black that shone and cast no shadow')

>> *It is hard to work out what is actually going on with regard to the light here. The strangeness of the image adds to the tension. The short sentence makes the image even starker.*

> *They stood over the omen like mourners.*

"You never know," Jess found herself saying, "It might be to protect it."

- Short paragraph
>> *Again, draws attention to the starkness of the image.*
- Simile ('like mourners')
>> *As well as capturing their confusion, this simile adds to the deathly imagery that surrounds the chain.*
- Direct speech
>> *Avoiding 'Jess said', I used the phrase 'Jess found herself saying' to suggest that she doesn't really know if she believes what she is saying.*

"
The sun had set. It was getting cold. The marble was now colliding with all the dark things kept at bay. It's times like these, Harsha thought, that you really needed a proper grown-up to tell you everything is going to be OK.

- Two short sentences in a row ('The sun had set. It was getting cold.')
>> *This really hammers home the glumness of the final image; the short sentences are bleak and cold.*

- Reference to earlier imagery ('The marble was now colliding')

>> *This is particularly high-level writing. If you can make use of a metaphor or simile that was introduced earlier in the story, you will show a real command of creative writing.*

- Reported thoughts

>> *The reported thoughts contrast nicely with the direct speech.*

EXEMPLAR PIECE FIVE
WRITE A FORMAL LETTER TO THE PRIME MINISTER ASKING FOR SCHOOL TO BE OPTIONAL

"Formal" is the key word with formal letter writing. This is your opportunity to show off your best words, your complex sentences, and your serious tone. Whatever happens, do not let your serious face slip. If what you are writing starts to sound a bit like how you would speak to your friends, change it.

Always remember:

- Dear ...
- A sign-off
- 'Yours sincerely', 'Regards', 'Yours truly', and 'Sincerely' are the most formal.
- An address

Letters are often written to persuade; in this case I am trying to persuade the Prime Minister to make school optional. As with all writing to persuade, it is a good idea to use many different points to make your argument. Three to four is usually a good number. Once you have decided on your points, then structure your paragraphs around your points. I have gone for the following structure:

1. Changing world
2. What is the point of school anyway?
3. Vocational jobs and manual labour
4. History

With formal letter writing, especially if you are trying to persuade someone, it is a good idea to state your argument as plainly as possible right at the start. This can just be a single sentence that sets out clearly your aims.

Formal language can take the form of interesting vocabulary, but it can also take the form of specific phrases. For example, it is a mark of formal writing to put prepositions before the word 'which': 'from which it was made'; 'out of which I climbed'; 'through which we suffer'. Other markers of formal language include 'thus', 'however', 'on the other hand', 'therefore', 'one' (used as a third-person pronoun), 'conversely', 'do so'.

10 Downing Street
London
SW1A 2AA
UK

Dear Mr. Johnson,

Following recent public discussions regarding the matter, we the undersigned[1] kindly request that the government cease demanding that children attend school up to the age of sixteen.

It is a travesty[2] that this country forces children into situations in which they would rather not be. We are a democracy that believes in liberty. We are a democracy that believes in the future. We are a democracy that learns from our past. Compulsory education has not rid our country of the difficulties from which it suffers, and so why would it do so in the years to come? We are living in a changing world that must learn to adapt to the challenges it faces. We sincerely believe that making formal education optional rather than mandatory is a step in the right direction.

School is important, we do not deny that. However, the arguments in favour of every single child attending school have simply run their course. What is the point of sending all children to educational establishments? So that all children can have the chance to progress to sixth form or college and then to university? What of all the jobs in this fine country that do not require a university education? Surely it would be better to train people early in these skilled professions rather than making them buy into a system that will only leave them in mounting debt?

It is time for Great Britain to celebrate vocational careers and manual labour; let children, and indeed their parents, choose the future of this country! Schools can instil a sense of failure in students who do not live up to the rigid expectations of a few arbitrary[3] subjects. If we were to celebrate craft, vocations, or even just the freedom of childhood expression, our future citizens would not carry with them outdated notions of intellectual failure, but rather take satisfaction in the life choices that they were allowed to make.

Across the world, the tyranny[4] of compulsory schooling is commonplace, but it was not always thus. There was once a time when people of this country passed their knowledge from parent to child, strengthening familial bonds. Medieval England saw generations of blacksmiths, of carpenters, of jewellers. Imagine what this did for the concept of community and belonging as knowledge was handed down the family line. Let us lead the way once again into this new dawn of education.

Yours sincerely,

Gregory Magnusson

(and the undersigned of Brompton Priory)

---

[1] **Undersigned** – *those who have signed this document*
[2] **Travesty** – *something awful; a distorted representation of something*
[3] **Arbitrary** – *based on random choice or personal whim*
[4] **Tyranny** – *cruel or oppressive rulership*

EXEMPLAR PIECE FIVE: GUIDANCE

Beginning

The beginning of a formal letter is probably the most formal part. You need the 'Dear ...', the address, and a short statement of intent. The more precise you are with the opening sentence, the more formal it will seem.

10 Downing Street
London
SW1A 2AA
UK

> *Dear Mr. Johnson,*
>
> *Following recent public discussions regarding the matter, we the undersigned kindly request that the government cease*

demanding that children attend school up to the age of sixteen.

- 'Dear ...,'
- Address
- Statement of intent
- Formal language ('we the undersigned', 'kindly request', 'cease demanding')

>> *If you want to make it seem like you are writing on behalf of a lot of people, 'we the undersigned', is a particularly good phrase to use.*

- 'Kindly request' is more formal than 'ask'.
- 'Cease' is more formal than 'stop'.

Middle

The main body of the letter sets out the argument. The points that I choose are broad and try to appeal to formal and serious matters like democracy, jobs, and freedom. You do not need to be as fusty as that, but it is a good idea to choose topics that are formal in this way.

EXEMPLAR PIECE FIVE: GUIDANCE / 67

> *It is a travesty that this country forces children into situations in which they would rather not be. We are a democracy that believes in liberty. We are a democracy that believes in the future. We are a democracy that learns from our past.*

- Formal language ('travesty', 'into situations in which')
- Tricolon ('We are a democracy [...] We are a democracy [...] We are a democracy')

> *Compulsory education has not rid our country of the difficulties from which it suffers, and so why would it do so in the years to come?*

- Formal language ('Compulsory education', 'from which it suffers', 'do so', 'years to come')
- Rhetorical question
>> *A rhetorical question is when you ask a question without expecting an answer for rhetorical effect.*
- Undermining the opposition argument
- Emotive language ('our country [...] suffers')
>> *The use of 'our' suggests collective responsibility for the suffering of the country.*

> *We are living in a changing world that must learn to adapt to the challenges it faces. We sincerely believe that making formal education optional rather than mandatory is a step in the right direction.*

- Directive statement ('a changing world that must learn')
>> *By using a directive statement that impels action, I create a sense of urgency.*
- Formal language ('sincerely', 'mandatory')
- First-person plural pronoun ('We')
>> *Gives a sense of collective duty as well as highlighting the number of people who have signed the letter.*
- Repetition of the main argument
>> *This hammers home the central point and gives a sense of authority.*

> *School is important, we do not deny that. However, the arguments in favour of every single child attending school have simply run their course.*

- Short sentence
>> *Makes the voice sound authoritative.*
- Formal language ('However', 'simply run their course')
- Acknowledging the positives of the opposition argument ('School is important')
>> *By acknowledging the positives of the opposition argument, and incorporating them into your own, you make your argument stronger.*

> *What is the point of sending all children to educational establishments? So that all children can have the chance to progress to sixth form or college and then to university? What of all the jobs in this fine country that do not require a university education? Surely it would be better to train people early in these skilled professions rather than making them buy into a system that will only leave them in mounting debt?*

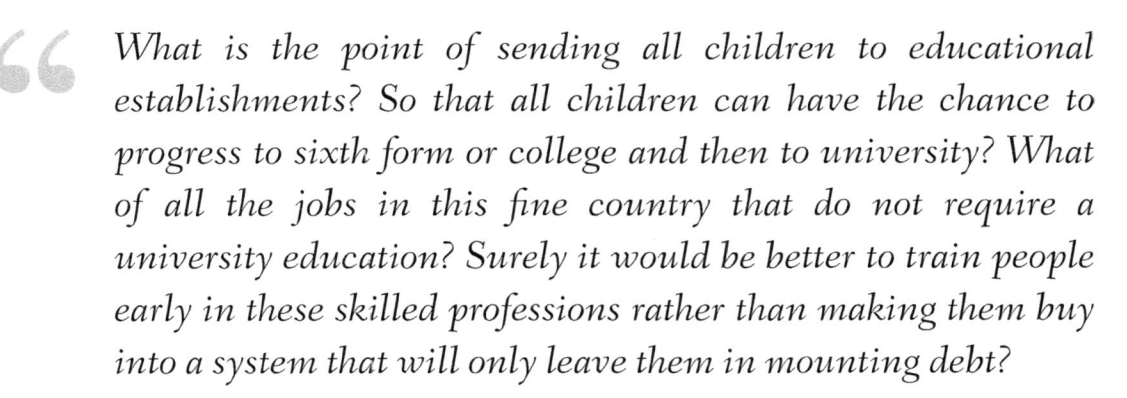

- Rhetorical questions
- Formal language ('educational establishments')

>> *If you are referring to the same thing many times, think of synonyms. This will really show off your vocabulary.*
- Emotive language ('this fine country')
>> *I have thought of who I am writing my letter to and appealed to a sense of national pride.*
- Making my argument the only reasonable argument ('Surely')
>> *Using the word 'surely' can present an argument as the only logical position.*

> *It is time for Great Britain to celebrate vocational careers and manual labour; let children, and indeed their parents, choose the future of this country!*

- Motivational language ('It is time')
- Punctuation use (';')
- Exclamation
>> *With formal letters, do not use exclamation marks too much. Once is probably enough (and only when you really need it).*

> *Schools can instil a sense of failure in students who do not live up to the rigid expectations of a few arbitrary subjects.*

- Dismissive tone ('a few arbitrary subjects')
>> *This subtle dismissal of the school curriculum strengthens the argument.*

> *If we were to celebrate craft, vocations, or even just the freedom of childhood expression, our future citizens would not carry with them outdated notions of intellectual failure, but rather take satisfaction in the life choices that they were allowed to make.*

- Complex, multi-clausal sentence
>> *A great big sentence like this is sure to impress anyone looking at the formality of your writing.*
>> *Look at how the sentence is constructed. 'If we were [...], or even just [...], then [...], but rather'; these are the important connecting phrases. Always think about*

whether you could turn a simple sentence or two into a complex sentence.
- Formal language ('If we were', 'future citizens', 'outdated notions of intellectual failure')

Ending

As I tie up the letter, I look at the wider picture. I think about how Britain relates to the rest of the world and to history. As ever, thinking about the wider perspective is a great way to end any piece of writing. Also, remember to include a formal sign off.

> *Across the world, the tyranny of compulsory schooling is commonplace, but it was not always thus.*

- Hyperbole ('tyranny')
>> *Using hyperbole can make the opposition argument seem terrible.*
>> *Hyperbole is another word for exaggeration.*
- Formal language ('commonplace', 'it was not always thus')

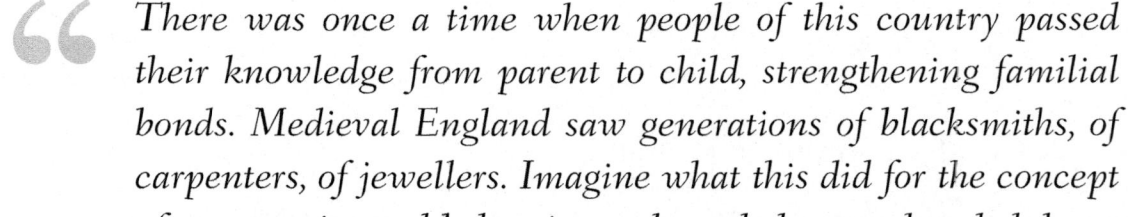

> *There was once a time when people of this country passed their knowledge from parent to child, strengthening familial bonds. Medieval England saw generations of blacksmiths, of carpenters, of jewellers. Imagine what this did for the concept of community and belonging as knowledge was handed down the family line.*

- Tricolon ('generations of blacksmiths, of carpenters, of jewellers')

EXEMPLAR PIECE FIVE: GUIDANCE / 73

- Imperative ('Imagine')

>> This is an attempt to speak directly to the reader.

" Let us lead the way once again into this new dawn of education.

- Rousing ending
- Hyperbole ('new dawn of education')

" Yours sincerely,

Gregory Magnusson

(and the undersigned of Brompton Priory)

- Formal sign off
- Included a reference to the 'undersigned'

A post box from the Victorian era!

EXEMPLAR PIECE SIX

YOU OWN A FOOTWEAR COMPANY. WRITE AN EMAIL TO SEND TO YOUR MAILING LIST PERSUADING THE READER TO BUY YOUR SHOES

Writing to persuade can take many forms. For this example, you are writing to sell a product. Advertising is often very informal, so you can use colloquialism, a low register, and you can even get away with improper sentences.

For advertising, you want to be snappy and sharp. You want to cover lots of different reasons why the reader should buy your product.

Sometimes the question will give you some information with which you can write your advertisement; sometimes it will not, and you will have to make something up.

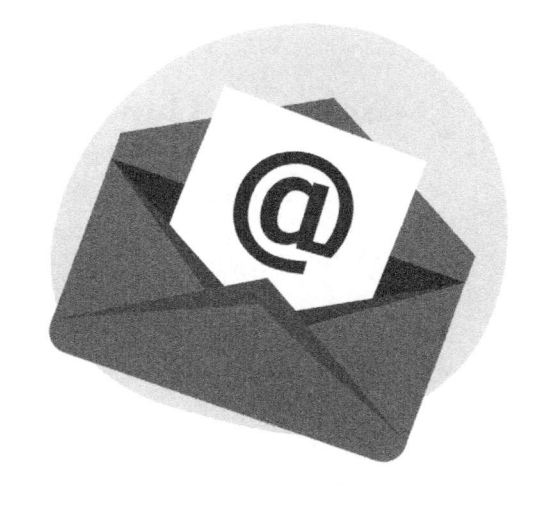

For this exercise, I have been asked to persuade a reader to buy some shoes. The first thing I have to think of is what sort of shoes. Try to envisage the product as best as you can, this will help you in the description.

Have a good think about the peritext of advertising. Peritext refers to things like titles, headings and subtitles – in other words, all the writing that doesn't make up the main body of your text. As this question asked me to write an email to a mailing list, I was sure to include a subject heading (in bold), a greeting, and a sign off.

I also experimented with short paragraphs, isolated quotations, and a final paragraph on the price and guarantee. The more things like this you include, the more you will show that you have really thought about the specifics of the question.

Humour is also recommended for advertising. Advertisers often find a way to make their writing entertaining; feel free to give it a go if ever you are asked to write to advertise a product.

> **Subject: These dogs definitely have sole**
>
> Hey Greg,
>
> Whether you're running away from your past or running towards a bright tomorrow, you'll do it faster with DogTrack trainers, the greyhounds of elite footwear.
>
> With their cutting-edge "wind slice" technology, DogTrack trainers glide through the air. You won't be caught off guard with these puppies on your feet. Three times comfier than the leading competitor, the new DT400s make your feet feel

like they're curling up by a crackling fire as you tear up the racetrack.

"I felt like I was running on air!"

- Shazmeen Naser, four-time Olympic medallist and world-record holder.

And, technically, she was. The DT400s are packed with a half-inch layer of hyper-compressed air sourced from the base camp of Mount Everest. Combined with unbeatable "wind slice" tech, this elite air gives the DT400s the spring you need to stay ahead of the pack.

That's not all ...

The DT400s, modelled by influencer and fashion icon, Perry Ames, recently featured on the front cover of *Yes That Please* magazine. These shoes look good. Coming in white, black, or granite grey, the DT400s boast a sleek strength in their minimalist design. The laces are fully customisable, and each purchase comes with spares.

These are trainers for all walks (or runs) of life: for those who want to stand out without making a scene; for those who want to push themselves beyond their limit; for those who want to savour every moment of the running experience; for those who want the best from life. The DT400s are for you.

At just £129.99, elite performance-wear could not come cheaper. With a no-questions-asked two-month guarantee, if you don't love them, you get your money back.

Remember DogTrack trainers are for life, not just for Christmas.

Till next time,

Rufus Rexton,

CEO DogTrack Footwear

EXEMPLAR PIECE SIX: GUIDANCE

Beginning

The beginning needs to be punchy. As well as including a subject heading and a greeting, I begin the email with a "mission statement". This mission statement has nothing to do with the product itself but communicates how I want the trainers to be seen. I have suggested that running is an important way of dealing with life's issues whilst also setting up the central theme of DogTrack trainers helping people to run like speedy dogs.

In the second paragraph, I lead with the unique selling point (USP) of the trainers whilst keeping up the dog-related imagery. You don't need to go too far when it comes to hamming up your central theme; I use much fewer dog-related puns as the email develops.

> ***Subject: These dogs definitely have sole***
>
> *Hey Greg,*
>
> *Whether you're running away from your past or running towards a bright tomorrow, you'll do it faster with DogTrack trainers, the greyhounds of elite footwear.*

- Subject heading
- Pun ('These dogs definitely have sole')
>> Punning is very common in advertising and can be a good way to entertain your reader.
- Second-person pronoun ('You')
>> Using the second-person pronoun draws the reader in and makes a connection between them and the product you are trying to sell.
- Metaphor ('the greyhounds of elite footwear')
>> As well as relating the trainers to an extremely fast animal, the metaphor explains the connection between the dogs and footwear.
- Synonym ('elite footwear')
>> This phrase makes trainers sound professional. Always be on the lookout for synonyms that can make something sound even more impressive.

EXEMPLAR PIECE SIX: GUIDANCE / 81

" *With their cutting-edge "wind slice" technology, DogTrack trainers glide through the air. You won't be caught off guard with these puppies on your feet. Three times comfier than the leading competitor, the new DT400s make your feet feel like they're curling up by a crackling fire as you tear up the racetrack.*

- Fronted adverbial ('With their cutting-edge "wind slice" technology')
>> *By leading with the adverbial phrase, I draw attention to the new technology.*
- Made-up jargon ('"wind slice" technology')
>> *Sometimes adverts will include jargon to make their products sound special. Feel free to make up jargon, as long as it is reasonably clear what you are talking about.*
>> *Jargon is specialised, often technical, vocabulary.*
- Pun ('with these puppies on your feet')
- Mention of competitor ('Three times comfier than the leading competitor')

>> *Distinguishing a brand from competing brands certainly makes you stand out.*
- Name of trainers ('DT400s')

>> *It gives a sense of reality to name the product.*
- Juxtaposition ('make your feet feel like they're curling up by a crackling fire as you tear up the racetrack')

>> *Juxtaposition is where you compare two very different or opposite things. Here, I have juxtaposed the cosiness of sitting by a fire with running fast around a racetrack. This accentuates just how cosy the trainers are.*

Middle

In the middle section, I start to think about the different ways to make the shoes seem attractive.

The two main angles that I went for were: elite sports and fashion. Brands often get famous people to endorse their products and so I made up two people, an athlete and an influencer, who could endorse the DT400s.

I presented the shift from athletics to fashions through a short sentence followed by an ellipsis ('That's not all ...'); this intrigues the reader and makes it clear through the visual separation, that there are different aspects to the trainers.

> *"I felt like I was running on air!"*
>
> *- Shazmeen Naser, four-time Olympic medallist and world-record holder.*

And, technically, she was. The DT400s are packed with a half-inch layer of hyper-compressed air sourced from the base camp of Mount Everest. Combined with unbeatable 'wind slice' tech, this elite air gives the DT400s the spring you need to stay ahead of the pack.

- Quotation ('I felt like I was running on air!')
>> *Quoting the words of a 'four-time Olympic medallist' gives the product legitimacy. Of course I am going to say that the trainers are good, I'm trying to sell them! Having a known athlete endorse them makes the trainers seem objectively good.*
- Starting a sentence with 'And' ('And, technically, she was.')
>> *Usually, it would not be considered good English to begin a sentence with a coordinating conjunction. However, when you are writing informally, it is fine to break these conventions.*
- Jargon ('half-inch layer of hyper-compressed air')
- Cliché ('the spring you need to stay ahead of the pack')
>> *A cliché is a commonplace phrase that is often used. In advertising clichés are used because they are familiar to readers. With this cliché, I have also managed to suggest a pack of dogs.*

INFLUENCE

> *That's not all ...*
>
> *The DT400s, modelled by influencer and fashion icon, Perry Ames, recently featured on the front cover of Yes That Please magazine. These shoes look good. Coming in white, black, or granite grey, the DT400s boast a sleek strength in their minimalist design. The laces are fully customisable, and each purchase comes with spares.*

- Short sentence and ellipsis ('That's not all ...')
>> *Gives a sense of separate sections to the email and accentuates the multifaceted nature of the trainers.*
- Mixture of short sentences and long sentences ('These shoes look good.')
>> *Mixing up the length of your sentences not only shows off your ability, but it also helps create a sense of rhythm to your writing, allowing emphasis to fall on specific phrases. In this case, the simplicity of the phrase suggests that little more needs to be said.*
- Alliteration ('granite grey')

>> *Referring to a surprising specification of colour is a method that is often used in advertising.*

> *These are trainers for all walks (or runs) of life: for those who want to stand out without making a scene; for those who want to push themselves beyond their limit; for those who want to savour every moment of the running experience; for those who want the best from life. The DT400s are for you.*

- Anaphoric list ('for those [...] for those [...] for those [...] for those')

>> *Anaphora is a technique that is usually associated with poetry, but it can also be applied to prose. It means the repetition of words or phrases at the beginning of a line, clause, or sentence. Here, the anaphora suggests that the DT400s are for many different types of people. I've chosen phrases that could appeal to just about anyone, whether they are an athlete or not.*

- Short sentence ('The DT400s are for you.')

>> *This is a very direct bit of advertising. Having gone through the list of people the trainers might be for, I single out the reader, and tell them squarely that the shoes are for them.*

Ending

Taking into account the transactional nature of the email, the ending refers to the nitty gritty details of the trainers: price and guarantee. Towards the end of any advertising task, be sure to think along these lines. It could be price, where the product is sold, whether there are any

86 / CREATIVE WRITING FOR KS3

discounts, that sort of thing. I also go back to the dog imagery to tie things up neatly.

> *At just £129.99, elite performance-wear could not come cheaper. With a no-questions-asked two-month guarantee, if you don't love them, you get your money back.*

- Price of the product
- Jargon ('elite performance-wear', 'no-questions-asked two-month guarantee')
- Hyperbole ('could not come cheaper')

> *Remember DogTrack trainers are for life, not just for Christmas.*

Till next time,

Rufus Rexton

CEO DogTrack Footwear

- Dog-related joke ('for life, not just for Christmas')
- Sign off
- Signature

EXEMPLAR PIECE SEVEN
WRITE A SPEECH TO GIVE TO YOUR CLASS ABOUT THE IMPORTANCE OF ART

Speechwriting is your chance to show off your rhetorical flair. You'll want to jam pack your speech with rousing sentences, rhetorical questions, and appeals to your audience. Read your writing out loud quietly or actively "speak" in your head. If it doesn't sound like speech, then change it.

One of the main things to remember about writing a speech is that the tone and register can be lowered slightly. Don't go too colloquial—this isn't a conversation between you and a friend—but do, for example, use contractions ('I'm', 'you're', 'don't'), the first-person pronoun, and informal language.

Do, also, take into account the audience of the speech. There is a difference between a speech given to your classmates and a speech given to a room full of politicians!

You will be rewarded for being alert to and demonstrating an awareness of your audience.

Feel free to make things up. Remember, while it helps to know a thing or two already about the topic you're writing about (in this case, art), you are ultimately being assessed on your speechwriting skills.

As ever, structure is important. You really want to grab your audience's attention at the beginning. Whether it's an anecdote, a joke, or a rhetorical question, try to go for a snappy opening. It is also good give a concise and precise thesis statement – that is, a bold statement that outlines your argument clearly.

Go big! Speeches are great for hyperbole and grand statements. Channel your inner Churchill, Pankhurst or Martin Luther King and inspire your audience. One particular technique that suits speeches really well is the rule of three (tricolon); I use it a lot.

> What comes to mind when I say the word "art"? Stuffy galleries? Pompous[1] elitism[2]? Meaningless scrawls of colour on a canvas that people pretend to like? Now, if that was all that "art" was about, I'd be the last person to sing its praises. There's nothing more I hate than people telling me that I should like some soulless, anodyne[3] painting because of an obscure theory or story that informs it. Whilst I'm sure that art of this kind has its place, I'm not advocating[4] for such rarefied[5] art today.

The art of Michelangelo, Matisse, Mondrian may well inspire you in a profound and earnest way. If so, that's amazing, nurture that inspiration! However, for many of you, high art might just leave you cold. And that is also fine. Today, I want us to divorce art from the gallery space, from the Masters, from the canvas. I want us to see art as something that's ongoing, that we're all a part of. I want us to see art as fundamental to the human condition.

The worst thing about art galleries is that they make you think of art as "out there", created by these genius artists who are nothing like us. This semi-religious ritual distances the individual from the art. We walk around a gallery thinking that we're not quite clever enough and not quite knowledgeable enough to appreciate it properly. But look, there is so much more to art than galleries: the pictures you take of you and your friends; the video games you play; the bits, bobs, and paraphernalia[6] that lie about your room; the placards you made to go on that march. This is all art. And I'd say that this art is way more important, way more radical, than a bunch of dying sunflowers painted in oil.

So, what makes something art and not just a part of everyday life? In a way, art is precisely what takes you out of everyday life. It's about looking at things from a different angle. Forget ideas of grandeur, riches, and being part of the long history of art; all you need to do to be an artist is to communicate something creative. This is why art is so inspirational for those who struggle to find a voice: those experiencing mental health crises; the marginalised; the introverted.

From the very first cave paintings to the doodles you're drawing at this very moment, art has always been a human impulse. We need art just as much as we need language; we need it to work out what on earth is going on in our heads. And so, yes, art is important. But we must remember that art is not there to show off how cultured you are. It is there to feel, to express, to sympathise, to scream, to scribble, to play, to love. Without art, we would lose our humanity.

---

[1] **Pompous** – *self-important, arrogant*
[2] **Elitism** – *the idea that some people are better than others*
[3] **Anodyne** – *dull, inoffensive, boring*
[4] **Advocating** – *arguing for*
[5] **Rarefied** – *distant from the concerns of ordinary people*
[6] **Paraphernalia** – *equipment used for a particular purpose*

EXEMPLAR PIECE SEVEN: GUIDANCE

Beginning

In the beginning, I really try to grab my audience's attention. I conjure a vivid description of the counterargument to what I will eventually go on to say. Here is a common argument for why art is pointless. By addressing this point and in fact agreeing with it in some way, my argument gains greater power.

I use lots of rhetorical questions and speech phrases. I make it personal, but I keep the overall argument clear.

In the second paragraph, I set out my argument plainly. A particularly strong rhetorical technique that I use in the second paragraph is the tricolon (three successive words, clauses, or sentences that can be seen as a group). The tricolon builds sentences into a crescendo and that is exactly what I do at the end of the paragraph, by beginning each sentence with the phrase 'I want us …'.

> *What comes to mind when I say the word "art"? Stuffy galleries? Pompous elitism? Meaningless scrawls of colour on a canvas that people pretend to like?*

- Rhetorical questions
- Speaking directly to the audience ('What comes to mind')
- Tricolon ('Stuffy galleries? Pompous elitism? Meaningless scrawls')

> *Now, if that was all that "art" was about, I'd be the last person to sing its praises. There's nothing more I hate than people telling me that I should like some soulless, anodyne painting because of an obscure theory or story that informs it. Whilst I'm sure that art of this kind has its place, I'm not advocating for such rarefied art today.*

- Speech phrase ('Now,')
- Use of the second-person pronoun

>> *This is also known as direct address.*

- Vocabulary ('anodyne', 'advocating', 'rarefied')
- Contractions ('I'm')

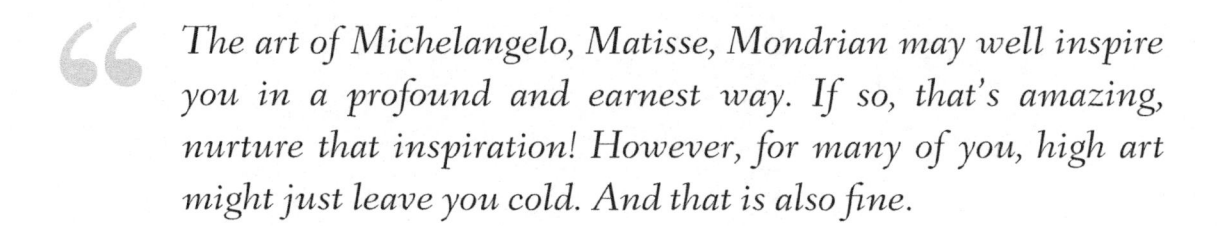

> *The art of Michelangelo, Matisse, Mondrian may well inspire you in a profound and earnest way. If so, that's amazing, nurture that inspiration! However, for many of you, high art might just leave you cold. And that is also fine.*

- Alliteration ('Michelangelo, Matisse, Mondrian')
- Reference to specific artists (these could also be made up)

>> *Speeches often refer to specific facts; try to include facts even if you need to make them up. Of course, made-up facts aren't technically facts at all, but we're making use of our poetic license.*

- Imperative ('nurture that inspiration!')

>> *An imperative tells the audience what to do and can be very powerful.*

- Informal language ('that's amazing', 'And that is also fine')
- Short sentence for effect ('And that is also fine')

> *Today, I want us to divorce art from the gallery space, from the Masters, from the canvas. I want us to see art as something that ongoing, that we're all a part of. I want us to see art as fundamental to the human condition.*

- Explicit statement of argument
>> *It is very important to be clear about the argument you are making early on in your speech.*
- Tricolon ('from the gallery space, from the Masters, from the canvas')
- Tricolon ('I want us to [...] I want us to [...] I want us to')
- First-person plural pronoun ('us', 'that we're all a part of')
>> *The use of the first-person plural pronoun helps to get the audience on side.*

Middle

The middle section gets deeper into the main argument, trying to get the audience to rethink their conception of art. It makes use of a list to give concrete examples of what art is and what art can be. Before the concrete examples, however, it speaks about art in the abstract. It can be a really good technique to alternate between abstract ideas and concrete examples.

There is a polemical element to the speech. A polemic is a piece of writing that is controversial and quite combative. My speech takes quite a strong stance against the idea of "elite" or "high" art. The reference to a 'bunch of dying sunflowers' tries to minimise the work of a famous artist called Vincent van Gogh.

Writing in the polemic style is a very bold choice; you would have to make sure that you tone down anything that might come across as a rant. However, especially when it comes to speech-writing, there's no harm in a bit of passionate argumentation.

> *The worst thing about art galleries is that they make you think of art as "out there", created by these genius artists who are nothing like us. This semi-religious ritual distances the individual from the art. We walk around a gallery thinking that we're not quite clever enough and not quite knowledgeable enough to appreciate it properly.*

- Slightly polemical style ('The worst thing about art galleries [...] these genius artists [...] This semi-religious')
- \>\> *The use of demonstrative pronouns ('these [...] This') can be a good way to create a sense of mockery.*
- In a speech you might use inverted commas to denote a difference in voice or tone ('"out there"')
- Hyperbole ('This semi-religious ritual')
- Repetition ('not quite clever enough and not quite knowledgeable enough')

EXEMPLAR PIECE SEVEN: GUIDANCE / 97

> *But look, there is so much more to art than galleries: the pictures you take of you and your friends; the video games you play; the bits, bobs, and paraphernalia that lie about your room; the placards you made to go on that march. This is all art.*

- Speech phrase ('But look')
- List
- Punctuation use (colons and semicolons in a list)
- Long sentence followed by short sentence

> *And I'd say that this art is way more important, way more radical, than a bunch of dying sunflowers painted in oil.*

- Intensification of statement ('way more important, way more radical,')

>> *This technique can really help your writing sound like speech; it is as if the speaker decides on a better phrase whilst they are speaking.*

> *So, what makes something art and not just a part of everyday life? In a way, art is precisely what takes you out of everyday life.*

- Rhetorical question and answering the rhetorical question.
>> *As I get to the end of the speech, I start to answer more questions than I ask. This gives a sense that a definite argument is being made.*

> *It's about looking at things from a different angle. Forget ideas of grandeur, riches, and being part of the long history of art; all you need to do to be an artist is to communicate something creative. This is why art is so inspirational for those who struggle to find a voice: those experiencing mental health crises; the marginalised; the introverted.*

- Tricolon ('grandeur, riches, and being part of the long history of art')
- Punctuation use (';')

- Punctuation use (colon to start a list and semicolons to separate items)
- Asyndeton and tricolon ('those experiencing mental health crises; the marginalised; the introverted.')

Ending

At the end of your speech, this is where you'll want to include a rousing climax. I do this mainly through the use of the list of verbs and the rather grand, though short, final sentence. It is also a good idea to link back to the opening of the speech, which I do by referring to 'show[ing] off how cultured you are.' Finally, it is quite a nice touch to address the audience directly, bringing them back into the speech.

> *From the very first cave paintings to the doodles you're drawing at this very moment, art has always been a human impulse.*

- Addressing the audience ('doodles you're drawing')
- Wider perspective ('very first cave paintings')
>> *Bringing in a wider perspective at the end here can give a sense that you have thought of how your speech relates to bigger issues.*

> *We need art just as much as we need language; we need it to work out what on earth is going on in our heads.*

- First-person plural pronoun ('We')
>> *This connects you to your audience.*

" *And so, yes, art is important. But we must remember that art is not there to show off how cultured you are.*

- Short sentence and speech phrase ('And so, yes, art is important.')
- Link back to the beginning ('to show off how cultured you are')

" *It is there to feel, to express, to sympathise, to scream, to scribble, to play, to love. Without art, we would lose our humanity.*

- Asyndeton ('to feel, to express, to sympathise, to scream')
- Grand final statement ('Without art, we would lose our humanity')

EXEMPLAR PIECE EIGHT
WRITE A NEWSPAPER ARTICLE ABOUT SOMETHING THAT HAPPENED IN YOUR LOCAL AREA

A NEWSPAPER ARTICLE is formal and factual. Sometimes you will be given some information to turn into a newspaper article, other times you will be asked to talk about something in your own life. As ever, if you are asked to write something about your own life, feel free to make it up. You are being marked on your ability to capture the style of a newspaper article.

Top tips for writing a newspaper article:

- Be specific
- Use times, dates, names, and titles.
- Use quotations
- Newspaper articles often include both long and short quotations.

- Cover multiple perspectives
- Try to think of different angles from which to approach the topic.
- Heading and subheadings
- This is a really good way of showing your awareness of the newspaper format.

In my article, I include a good number of quotations. This gives the impression that it is not me as the writer who has opinions about the issue, but rather the people speaking. I have also tried to capture the voice of the speakers.

All of the advice in this chapter could also be used if you were asked to write something for a blog or a magazine; however, for these formats your writing can be slightly more informal.

Newspaper articles do not tend to use florid language, neither do they tend to use complex sentences. Being clear and concise is key.

> ### TROUBLE IN PARADISE
>
> Revellers Cause Havoc in Peaceful Neighbourhood
>
> **A Rude Awakening**
>
> At 2am on Friday 14th May, residents of Bagnor Close in north Wigginsworth awoke to the sounds of lorries, drills, shouting, and thumping music. Overnight, this quiet, elderly neighbourhood had been transformed into a "radical performance space". By 9:30am, a sea of stalls, tents, and

stages swamped the whole cul-de-sac[1]. The first guests arrived an hour later.

This is not the first time that the residents of Bagnor Close have had run-ins with "guerrilla[2] festivals". Situated at Wigginsworth's highest point and boasting some of the best views of the town's world-famous scenery, the spot consistently ranks in the top five best streets in Britain. However, that plaudit[3] comes at a price; this was the sixth unlicensed event that has been held at Bagnor Close in the past two years.

Frustrated Locals

Margaret Deaney, long-term resident and Neighbourhood Watch Coordinator has had enough of the nuisance:

"I just don't know how people can be so selfish. How would they like it if we turned up at their houses in the middle of the night and banged on their door all weekend? Either they are completely oblivious[4] to us as people, or—and I hate to think people could be so cruel—or they know we don't want them here and they simply don't care!"

The local council has called the events "reprehensible"[5], but residents are complaining that they have had no support in stopping the festival returning. Some, like churchwarden Samuel Waterson, are looking elsewhere for the peace and quiet that had drawn them to Bagnor Close in the first place:

"I've had enough. I'm sorry, I've had enough. The last time my front window was smashed by a particularly well wanged welly. Now I know it's all a bit of fun like, but it's not fun for me. I tell you. This is my life. I'm selling up, getting out of here."

Bored Youths

As the tents were packed away on Sunday evening, we managed to speak to one of the organisers of Tomorrow is Ours Festival and asked her about the sufferings of local residents:

"I mean, you're always going to get push back. Nimbyism[6], isn't it? At the end of the day, they just don't like us because we're young. They're more than welcome to get involved if they want to; but they don't."

In the past three months, there has been a 58% rise in illegal gatherings in suburban areas throughout the UK, mostly attended by those aged 16-30. The People's Doings Institute, a national independent think tank[7], has suggested that neglect in youth culture has forced young people to take matters into their own hands, especially outside of urban hubs.

At 6:30am on Monday morning, Margaret Deaney and her team of volunteers spent six hours cleaning up the sea of litter and discarded tents left by the weekend's revellers. Now, they wait in dread for what this weekend will bring.

---

[1] ***Cul-de-sac*** – *Street with a dead end*
[2] ***Guerrilla*** – *impromptu activity; originally referring to warfare*
[3] ***Plaudit*** – *recognition, acclaim, or applause*
[4] ***Oblivious*** – *unknowing*
[5] ***Reprehensible*** – *disgraceful*

⁶ ***Nimbyism*** – NIMBY, *acronym for 'not in my back yard'*
⁷ ***Think tank*** – *a research organisation that advises on things like culture, economics, the military, technology, and politics*

Ask a parent or a guardian to get you a newspaper: it's a great way to start familiarising yourself with the journalistic tone! Copyright © VV Nincic

EXEMPLAR PIECE EIGHT: GUIDANCE

Beginning

The first thing to think about for your newspaper article is a heading. Make it big and make it catchy.

Below your main heading, you might have a smaller heading that explains in more detail the topic of the article. Then you should choose between three and four subheadings, which will separate the article into different sections. This can help you to make sure that you are approaching the topic from different angles.

I chose the made-up topic of revellers in a cul-de-sac because it would allow me to have quotations from different people whilst also allowing me to focus on facts and figures.

A great article will have a mixture of human opinion and facts. I start with the event, being as specific as I can, and then move to the wider ramifications.

> TROUBLE IN PARADISE
>
> Revellers Cause Havoc in Peaceful Neighbourhood

- Headings
>> *The first heading is bigger, vaguer and shorter; the second is longer and more specific. This is a good template to use for headings.*

> ***A Rude Awakening***
>
> *At 2am on Friday 14th May, residents of Bagnor Close in north Wigginsworth awoke to the sounds of lorries, drills, shouting, and thumping music.*

- Subheading

>> *Keep the subheadings short, usually just an adjective and a noun.*
- Specifics ('2am on Friday 14th May, residents of Bagnor Close in north Wigginsworth')

>> *It is good to mention the time, date, and location in the first sentence. Imagine you are a newsreader giving the most important information first.*

- List ('lorries, drills, shouting, and thumping music')

>> *This list of noises accentuates the nuisance of the festival, suggesting that the author sides with the residents.*

"*Overnight, this quiet, elderly neighbourhood had been transformed into a "radical performance space". By 9:30am, a sea of stalls, tents, and stages swamped the whole cul-de-sac. The first guests arrived an hour later.*

- Quotation marks ('"radical performance space"')

>> *By putting this phrase in quotation marks, it seems as though I am using the specific terminology of the festival organisers.*

- Metaphor and tricolon ('a sea of stalls, tents, and stages')

>> *Metaphor is not often used in newspaper writing but in this case it emphasises just how much is cluttering up the cul-de-sac.*

- The tricolon similarly suggests excess
- Short sentence ('The first guests arrived an hour later')

>> *Newspaper articles often use short, simple sentences.*

" *This is not the first time that the residents of Bagnor Close have had run-ins with "guerrilla festivals". Situated at Wigginsworth's highest point and boasting some of the best views of the town's world-famous scenery, the spot consistently ranks in the top five best streets in Britain. However, that plaudit comes at a price; this was the sixth unlicensed event that has been held at Bagnor Close in the past two years.*

- Quotation marks ("guerrilla festivals")

>> *Again, this unattributed quotation makes it obvious that*

> *this is a new term, perhaps one made up by the organisers.*
- Formal language ('boasting', 'world-famous', 'consistently')
>> *This is the language of journalism accentuating the spot's beauty.*
- Vocabulary ('plaudit')
- Punctuation use (';')

Middle

Having reported the news event and explained its context, the middle section focuses on the opinions of the residents.

I decided to focus on two residents: one who is in a position of responsibility and another who wants to leave. In my quotations, I have thought about how to recreate voice through the use of colloquial phrases and non-standard English. By focusing on the opinions of the locals, I have given the story more of a human edge and helped the reader to understand exactly what they are suffering.

> ### *Frustrated Locals*
>
> *Margaret Deaney, long-term resident and Neighbourhood Watch Coordinator, has had enough of the nuisance:*

- Subheading
- Full name and occupation ('Margaret Deaney, long-term resident and Neighbourhood Watch Coordinator')
>> *This is a great template for introducing interviewees and is particular to the newspaper article format.*
- Punctuation use (':')

> "I just don't know how people can be so selfish. How would they like it if we turned up at their houses in the middle of the night and banged on their door all weekend? Either they are completely oblivious to us as people, or—and I hate to think people could be so cruel—or they know we don't want them here and they simply don't care!"

- Emotive language ('I just don't know')
- Rhetorical question ('How would they like it...?')
- Punctuation use ('–')
>> *The use of the em dash here gives the impression of broken speech.*
- Repetition ('or')
>> *Again, the repetition of 'or' makes this sound more like speech than writing.*
- Exclamation ('and they simply don't care!')
>> *Always best to be wary of exclamations, but when you are recreating the voice of a character who is showing lots of emotion, go for it!*

> *The local council has called the events "reprehensible", but residents are complaining that they have had no support in stopping the festival returning. Some, like churchwarden Samuel Waterson, are looking elsewhere for the peace and quiet that had drawn them to Bagnor Close in the first place:*

- Another shift in perspective ('The local council')
- Vocabulary ('reprehensible')
- Full name and occupation ('churchwarden Samuel Waterson')

> *"I've had enough. I'm sorry, I've had enough. The last time my front window was smashed by a particularly well wanged welly. Now I know it's all a bit of fun like, but it's not fun for me. I tell you. This is my life. I'm selling up, getting out of here."*

- Colloquial tone ('I've had enough. I'm sorry, I've had enough', 'well wanged welly', 'it's all a bit of fun like')
- Short sentences

\>\> *The short sentences give a sense of the man's frustration.*

Ending

Finally, I get round to the perspective of the festival organisers. It is always a really good idea to listen to both sides of the story, even if you are ultimately going to be presenting one in a more favourable light than the other.

I also bring in some wider statistics. Again, statistics (even if they are made up) are a good thing to get into your newspaper article somewhere as they give the impression of authority.

I end the article with the image of Mrs. Deaney clearing up the rubbish of the festival in order to be clear that the article does not endorse the behaviour of the festivalgoers. It is an image that makes you feel sympathy for her.

" *Bored Youths*

As the tents were packed away on Sunday evening, we managed to speak to one of the organisers of Tomorrow is Ours Festival and asked her about the sufferings of local residents.

"I mean, you're always going to get push back. Nimbyism, isn't it? At the end of the day, they just don't like us because we're young. They're more than welcome to get involved if they want to; but they don't."

- Use of first-person plural pronoun ('we')
>> *This suggests that the author is part of a reporting team at the festival.*
- Naming the festival
>> *Gives a sense of realism.*
- Colloquial tone ('I mean', 'isn't it?', 'At the end of the day')
- Vocabulary ('Nimbyism')
>> *'Nimbyism' is a strange word derived from the acronym NIMBY (Not In My Back Yard). Those accused of nimbyism don't want to see anything built or organised in their neighbourhood.*
- Punctuation use (';')

> *In the past three months, there has been a 58% rise in illegal gatherings in suburban areas throughout the UK, mostly attended by those aged 16-30. The People's Doings Institute, a national independent think tank, has suggested that neglect in youth culture has forced young people to take matters into their own hands, especially outside of urban hubs.*

- Statistics
- National perspective

>> *If you are reporting on something local, always good to take a moment to think of the national/international perspective.*

- Taking time to think of the reasons for the crimes
- Vocabulary ('think tank)
- Jargon ('urban hubs')

>> *I recommend reading some newspapers and taking note of journalistic language.*

> *At 6:30 on Monday morning, Margaret Deaney and her team of volunteers spent six hours cleaning up the sea of litter and*

discarded tents left by the weekend's revellers. Now, they wait in dread for what this weekend will bring.

- Ending on a note of sympathy for the residents
- Reuse of earlier metaphor ('sea of litter and discarded tents')
- Change in tense ('Now they wait in dread')

>> *This reiterates the idea that it is an ongoing situation.*

LANGUAGE TECHNIQUES AND TECHNICAL TERMS

Addressing the audience – a useful way to keep an audience engaged
From the very first cave paintings to the doodles you're drawing at this very moment.

Alliteration – repetition of consonants
Clickity clack on the spotless streets.

Ambiguity – when something is open to interpretation
He stood tall, threw his head back, opened his mouth wide, and screamed at the falling rain.

Anaphora – repetition of a word or phrase at the start of a line or sentence
For those who want to stand out without out making a scene; for those who want to push themselves beyond their limit; for those who want to savour every moment of the running experience; for those who want the best from life.

Anti-climax – building tension without there being a climax
It lingered, lowered its head slightly, turned and sauntered away.

Aphoristic – a very short statement that contains universal truth
There's always something new to say on a walk

Aposiopesis – breaking off mid-speech or mid-sentence
"What is—Jess, come, have a look at this!"

Asyndeton – the use of lots of commas instead of conjunctions
The cake was just beyond the next bluff, down the hill, around the reservoir.

Authorial insertion – when the narrator reveals themselves as a writer
That and the intellectual fire from our very important conversation about—I can't remember what—that had begun as soon as we left the car and was still raging.

Balanced phrasing – using similar sentence structures close together
As the sun fell, so the shadows grew.

Characterisation – making different characters behave in different ways
Harsha was taking a stroll around the edge of the oak, taking in the impermeant gold of the evening while Jess was adding foliate borders to their hallowed document.

Colloquial language – conversational, informal language
It's all a bit of fun like.

Complex sentences – a sentence with lots of clauses is good for formal and creative writing
They had spent the afternoon helping the farmer stack hay and, though the

heat and the work drove them nearly to exhaustion, the changing air was now filling them with a feeling they had experienced on many a long summer's evening, but at this moment felt indescribably new.

Compound word – a new word made by linking two words together with a hyphen
Walk-running

Contractions – turning two words into one
Don't [...] I'm [...] Haven't

Counterargument – the opposite argument to the one that you are making
What comes to mind when I say the word "art"? Stuffy galleries? Pompous elitism? Meaningless scrawls of colour on a canvas that people pretend to like?

Delayed revelation – waiting till further on in your writing to reveal information
Asleep, or breakfasting, or doing whatever it is that humans do in the mornings, the inhabitants of this antiquated town will miss the unremarkable drama of a crisp packet being swept up.

Demonstrative pronouns – can be used to create a sense of mockery
The worst thing about art galleries is that they make you think of art as "out there", created by these genius artists who are nothing like us. This semi-religious ritual distances the individual from the art

Direct speech – quoted speech; use sparingly
"Copy. I hear you loud and –"

Directive statement – a statement that suggests action
We are living in a changing world that must learn to adapt to the challenges it faces.

Emotive language – language that tries to make the reader feel emotions
What of all the jobs in this fine country that do not require a university education?

Focus on senses – attention to sights, smells, sounds, feelings, and taste
He was panting heavily, thirsty and tired. As Patroller 35701 turned her head from the hot stench of his heavy breathing, she thought she heard him growl something that sounded uncannily like, "Leave. Me. Alone!"

Formal language – big words and complex sentence structure; no colloquialisms
Dear Mr. Johnson,

Following recent public discussions regarding the matter, we the undersigned kindly request that the government cease demanding children to go to school up to the age of sixteen.

Focus on the weather – highly recommended for fiction writing
The red sun, still low in the one chunk of unclouded sky, blinded her as she stumbled to the window.

Fronted adverbial – a phrase at the start of a sentence that describes an action
From where I lie, the timeless town looms rigidly.

Heading – a big title to be used in newspaper writing
TROUBLE IN PARADISE

Revellers Cause Havoc in Peaceful Neighbourhood

Hyperbole – exaggeration
Across the world, the tyranny of compulsory schooling is commonplace, but it was not always thus.

Imagery – using language associated with one thing to describe something else
Disordered, they paint a living picture across the neat and clean and tidy town; they caw, they flutter, they make a mess on the sterile streets and the deathly sky. Some call them harbingers of death, but I see them as hardy cackles of life.

Imperative – a command
Nurture that inspiration!

Informal tone – writing that sounds more like speech, sometimes with non-standard English
And, technically, she was.

Jargon – specialised vocabulary
With their cutting-edge 'wind slice' technology, DogTrack trainers glide through the air.

Juxtaposition – putting two opposing or clashing images or ideas next to each other
Three times comfier than the leading competitor, the new DT400s make your feet feel like they're curling up by a crackling fire as you tear up the racetrack.

Made up names and places – gives life to creative writing

In the concrete badlands of Greater Siltington, West Saxonbury, life was scarce.

Metaphor – saying that one thing is another thing or that
Husks of an ancient civilisation tottered on bending beams that had been threatening to snap for decades.

Onomatopoeia – recreating a sound in writing
Thunk

Originality – when something is interesting, unexpected, or surprisingly described
It was hard to tell where the shadows ended and the beast began.

Peritext – that which goes around the main body of writing
These dogs definitely have sole

Personification – giving human characteristics to something non-human
The forest that had waited patiently all this time for us to shut up and listen.

Polysyndeton – using lots of conjunctions instead of punctuation
They laughed and hid and chased and argued and arrived.

Pun – a joke made through double-meaning
With these puppies on your feet.

Register – your choice of words; you can have high register and low register
High register – *Across the world, the tyranny of compulsory schooling is commonplace, but it was not always thus.*
Low register – *But look, there is so much more to art than galleries.*

Repetition – repeating things can be used for narrative effect
Second by second, moment by moment.

Rhetorical question – a question that does not expect an answer
What is the point of sending all children to educational establishments?

Setting the scene – take time to set the scene in creative writing
The forest glistened with snow on the cusp of melting. Occasionally, great chunks would slide and fall from the branches of pines, creating little undramatic snowfalls above our heads.

Shift in focus – a movement from one location or time to another
Asleep, or breakfasting, or doing whatever it is that humans do in the mornings...

Shift in perspective – a movement to a different character's point of view
Suddenly we saw ourselves from the forest's point of view, the forest that had waited patiently all this time for us to shut up and listen.

Shift in tone – a movement from a certain narrative style to a different narrative style
They stood over the omen like mourners.

Sign off – what you write at the end of a letter
Yours sincerely,

Simile – saying something is 'like' something else or 'as ...' as something else
Like a pair of busy mice, squeaking to each other through the undergrowth, we weaved through the forest trail.

Statistics – facts can be particularly useful in newspaper writing
In the past three months, there has been a 58% rise in illegal gatherings in suburban areas throughout the UK, mostly attended by those aged 16-30.

Subheading – a smaller title that you should use about 3 or 4 of in newspaper writing
A Rude Awakening

Subordinate clause – a clause whose meaning is dependent on the main clause
If we were to celebrate craft, vocations, or even just the freedom of childhood expression...

Sympathy (pathos) – making a reader feel sympathy for a character is a good idea
On Monday morning, Margaret Deaney leads a team of volunteers and cleans up the sea of litter and discarded tents left by the weekend's revellers.

Synonym – another word for the same thing
Elite footwear

Syntax – sentence structure; it is good to vary your syntax
Distant clouds thickened. He watched the human clamber over rubble and old pipes, scanning the building as she came closer, ever closer. For five days now, he had been sheltering from the unrelenting sun without food, without water. He was usually much better at boulder-hurling.

Tension – the feeling that something is about to happen
Rain started to fall. She had been scanning for an hour and was only on the fourteenth floor. "Patroller 35701. Come in Patroller 35701," a crackled voice hissed in her ear.

Thesis statement – a brief declaration of a main argument
Following recent public discussions regarding the matter, we the undersigned kindly request that the government cease demanding children to go to school up to the age of sixteen.

Tone – the general feel of a piece of writing created through language techniques
No one wanted to survey the badlands, but Patroller 35701 was the kind of person who got the jobs that no one wanted to do

Tricolon (rule of three) – a list of three words or phrases
They caw, they flutter, they make a mess on the sterile streets and the deathly sky.

Voice – the character of the narrator, revealed through phrases and opinions
A change in scenery can do that, you know; there's always something new to say on a walk.

Printed in Great Britain
by Amazon